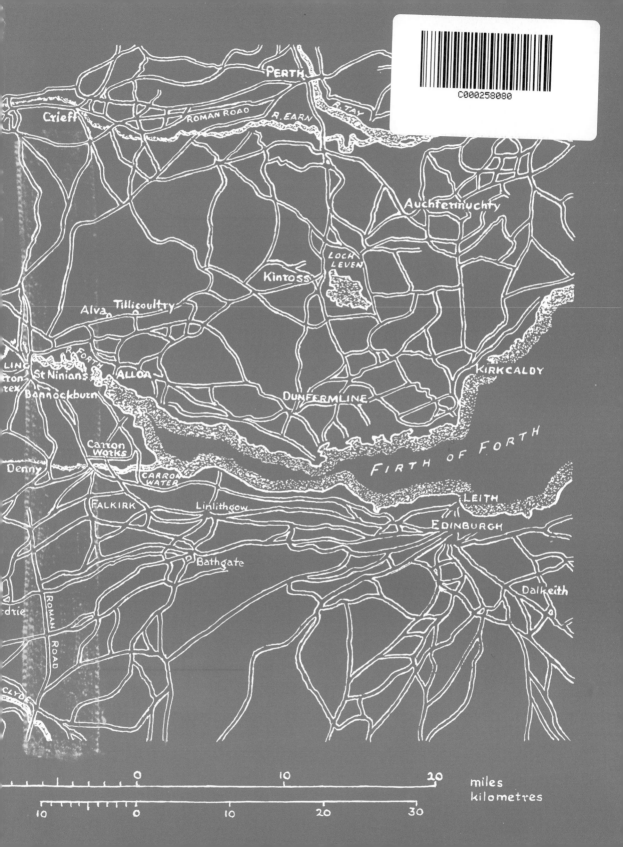

THE RAILWAY CARRIERS

Belfast Address—
38-40 WARING STREET

Dublin Address—
2 BERESFORD PLACE

WORDIE & CO.

A. WATSON.
W. WORDIE.

GENERAL CARRIERS, RAILWAY, SHIPPING, AND FORWARDING AGENTS,

WAREHOUSE-KEEPERS
AND
CARTING CONTRACTORS
Agents for

Scottish Branches
ABERDEEN
ARBROATH
DUNDEE
EDINBURGH
INVERNESS
LEITH
PERTH
STIRLING, Etc.

English and Irish Branches
NEWCASTLE-ON-TYNE
BELFAST
DUBLIN
LONDONDERRY
ARMAGH
DROGHEDA
NEWRY
DUNDALK, Etc.

LONDON MIDLAND AND SCOTTISH RAILWAY COMPANY and GREAT NORTHERN RAILWAY (Ireland)

AND IN CONNECTION WITH ALL THE PRINCIPAL RAILWAYS AND SHIPPING COMPANIES

CHIEF OFFICES—
75 WEST NILE STREET, GLASGOW

GLASGOW
NOVEMBER, 1929.

Telegraphic Address—"WORDIES"

CARTING AGENTS FOR LONDON MIDLAND AND SCOTTISH RAILWAY COMPANY, 63 MELBOURNE STREET, NEWCASTLE-ON-TYNE.

ARRIVALS OF STEAMERS
FOREIGN

From BALTIMORE
s.s. "BANNACK," - - 5th Nov.
s.s. "BELHAVEN," - 12th Nov.
s.s. "BALSAM." - 18th Nov.
s.s. "WEST ALSEK," 26th Nov.

From PACIFIC PORTS
m.v. "PACIFIC PRESIDENT," 13th Nov.
m.v. "PACIFIC ENTERPRISE," 22nd Nov.

From BOSTON
NOTHING FIXED

From MONTREAL and QUEBEC
T.s.s. "MINNEDOSA," - 3rd Nov.
T.s.s. "CARMIA," - 5th Nov.
T.s.s. "LETITIA," 10th Nov.
T.s.s. "MELITA," 17th Nov.
s.s. "CORINALDO," 19th Nov.
T.s.s. "ATHENIA," 24th Nov.
T.s.s. "CARMIA" 3rd Dec.

From NEW YORK
s.s. "BANNACK," 5th Nov.
T.s.s. "CAMERONIA," 10th N.
s.s. "BELLHAVEN," 12th N.
T.s.s. "TRANSYLVANIA," 7th Nov.
s.s. "BALSAM," 18th Nov.
T.s.s. "CALEDONIA," 24th Nov.
s.s. "WEST ALSEK," 26th Nov.

From NEW ORLEANS
s.s. "WEST COBALT," 4th Nov.
s.s. "WEST HOBONAC," 24th Nov.
s.s. "WEST CADDOA," 7th Dec.

From PHILADELPHIA
NOTHING FIXED

From SAVANNAH
NOTHING FIXED

DEPARTURES OF STEAMERS
FOREIGN

To ADELAIDE, MELBOURNE, SYDNEY, BRISBANE
s.s. "NINGCHOW," 6th Nov.
s.s. "DELPHIC," 13th Nov.
s.s. "NESTOR," 27th Nov.
s.s. "RUNIC." 4th Dec.

To AUCKLAND, WELLINGTON, PORT CHALMERS, LYTTLETON
T.s.s. "RIMUTAKA," 14th Nov.
T.s.s. "HORORATA," 26th Nov.

To BOSTON
NOTHING FIXED

To BOMBAY
s.s. "HARMONIDES," 5th Nov.
s.s. "CITY OF CALCUTTA," 9th Nov.
s.s. "MASSILIA," 15th Nov.
STEAMER, 22nd Nov.
s.s. "CASTALIA," 29th Nov.

To ALGOA BAY, EAST LONDON
s.s. "ASTRONOMER," 7th Nov.
STEAMER, - 28th Nov.

To CALCUTTA
s.s. "MANGALORE," 5th Nov.
s.s. "CITY OF BENARES," 9th Nov.
s.s. "CLAN OGILVIE," 14th Nov.
s.s. "MALANCHA," 14th Nov.
STEAMER, 28th Nov.

To FREMANTLE
s.s. "DELPHIC," 13th Nov.
s.s. "NESTOR," 27th Nov.

To KARACHI
s.s. "CITY OF CALCUTTA," 9th Nov.
s.s. "MASSILIA," 15th Nov.
s.s. "CITY OF LAHORE," 25th Nov.
s.s. "CASTALIA." 29th Nov.

To NEW YORK
T.s.s. "CALEDONIA," 2nd Nov.
T.s.s. "CAMERONIA," 16th Nov.
T.s.s. "TRANSYLVANIA," 23rd Nov.
T.s.s. "CALEDONIA." 30th Nov.

To NATAL, DELAGOA BAY
s.s. "ASTRONOMER," 7th Nov.
s.s. "CLAN MACKINLAY," 21st Nov.
STEAMER, 23rd Nov.

To PHILADELPHIA
NOTHING FIXED

To QUEBEC and MONTREAL
T.s.s. "ATHENIA," 1st Nov.
T.s.s. "CARMIA," 8th Nov.
T.s.s. "MINNEDOSA," 9th Nov.
T.s.s. "LETITIA," 15th Nov.
T.s.s. "CORINALDO," 25th Nov.

To SAN FRANCISCO, SEATTLE, VANCOUVER, PORTLAND, ORE.
m.v. "PACIFIC PIONEER," 11th Nov.
m.v. "PACIFIC PRESIDENT," 25th Nov.

To RANGOON
s.s. "KEMMENDINE," 13th Nov.
s.s. "SAGAING." 27th Nov.

COASTWISE STEAMERS

BELFAST
BURNS & LAIRD LINES Ltd. Daily Service
(Except Sundays)

BRISTOL
WM. SLOAN & CO. Mons. & Thurs.

CARDIFF, SWANSEA & NEWPORT (Mon.)
WM. SLOAN & CO. Fridays.

DUBLIN
BURNS & LAIRD LINES Ltd. Daily Service
(Except Sundays)

LONDONDERRY
BURNS & LAIRD LINES Ltd.
Mondays, Tuesdays, Wednesdays, Fridays, Saturdays.

MANCHESTER
COAST LINES Ltd.
(BURNS & LAIRD LINES Ltd., Agents)
Every Saturday.

LIVERPOOL
COAST LINES Ltd.
(BURNS & LAIRD LINES Ltd., Agents)
Tuesdays* and Saturdays.
* Alternate Wednesdays.

ROBERT GILCHRIST & CO.
Wednesdays and Saturdays.

LONDON
CLYDE SHIPPING CO., Ltd.
Tuesdays, Wednesdays, and Fridays.

WATERFORD
CLYDE SHIPPING CO., Ltd.
Mondays and Wednesdays.

N.B.—Owing to existing conditions, the Dates of Sailings and Arrivals may be altered or cancelled, and we cannot accept responsibility for any inaccuracies which may appear on this List

We have an experienced Staff, and Bills of Lading Orders, Forwarding and Shipping Instructions, Customs Clearances, etc., receive prompt and careful attention

THE RAILWAY CARRIERS

The history of Wordie & Co., Carriers, Hauliers
and Store Keepers, as told to and illustrated by

EDWARD PAGET-TOMLINSON

Edward Paget-Tomlinson

You'll find Wordie & Co.
wherever you go

TERENCE DALTON LIMITED
in conjunction with
THE WORDIE PROPERTY COMPANY LIMITED 1990

Published by
TERENCE DALTON LIMITED
in conjunction with
THE WORDIE PROPERTY COMPANY LIMITED

ISBN 0 86138 082 7

Text photoset in 10/11pt Baskerville

Printed in Great Britain at
The Lavenham Press Limited, Lavenham, Suffolk
© Edward Paget-Tomlinson, 1990

Contents

Dedicated to everyone
who worked with
Wordie & Co.

Foreword

WHEN we decided to prepare this history of a family business, our aims were modest: to tell from the available documents the story of a firm which became a household name in Scotland, Ireland and the North of England.

To introduce a human note, we decided to ask for the help of former Wordie employees and their relatives; the response was overwhelming, not only from those near at hand but also from further afield—Canada, the United States of America, Australia and South Africa.

So productive have our correspondents been that instead of a bald family company history we have been able to assemble a first-hand record of a road carrier's business, dominated by the horse and only mechanized in the last few decades of its life.

Contributions have come from over 120 people, and our cousin Edward Paget-Tomlinson, who at inception took on the role of author, ended up more as editor and, we hasten to add, illustrator.

The final product can now be seen and assessed: we hope that you, the reader, derive some interest and pleasure from its pages.

John S. Wordie
George T. Wordie
Peter J. Wordie

Uncle John
Uncle George.

Charles

Acknowledgements

THIS history has been the work of many people. It could not have been written had not more than 120 members of Wordie & Co. and their relatives come forward with their recollections, which go back to the nineteen-twenties and sometimes a bit earlier, and when speaking of their parents to the nineteen-hundreds. Here is everyone, in alphabetical order:

G. Adam, Cecil Allen, Tom Atkin, OBE, Irvine Barton,. William Binnie, William Birse, Mrs Caroline B. Bourner, Alexander Brechin, Leslie H. Brown, Mrs Helen Bruce, Norman Bruce, Mrs A. Burnside, Alan D. Campbell, Mrs Mary Cassie, Duncan Chisholm, Mrs Margaret Coulin, Mrs N. Coulston, Mrs T. Crawford, Mrs Sheena Crook, Robert Davey, George A. Dey, the Misses Dickson, Raymond Eddie, John Elliot, Mrs Mary Ferguson, George S. Findlater, Miss Anne Forbes, Alexander Forsyth, Miss E. A. Fraser, Robert Fulton, James P. Fyfe, Joe Galway, Miss Mary Galway, Miss Elsie M. Gibson, Peter Giffen, Iain J. Gilchrist, Mrs Mary Gillespie, Mrs N. Gilliland, Adam Gilmour, Walter M. Gowans, Dr R. F. Gracey, MRCVS, E. Graham, Mr and Mrs Hugh Gray, Margaret E. H. Gray, Mrs S. Greenan, Fred Gunn, A. D. Hamilton, Stewart Hamilton, W. H. Hamp-Hamilton, Stan Harrison, Fred Hawkins, William Henderson, James Hendry, Mrs D. Henzell, W. Heuchan, Jackie Hogg, Jack House, R. G. Ireland, R. J. Ironside, Joe Johannsen, Jim Keenan, Dr M. Kelly, R. W. Kirkpatrick, MRCVS, Douglas Knox, Herbert Knox, Mrs M. Leishman, Robert Lewis, Otto Lippart, David C. Lochrie, William Lorimer, Ian MacBean, Eddie McCaffery, R. M. McCaughey, MRCVS, Bertie McClintock, Hector MacDonald, Archie McGill, Miss Helen McGregor, Mrs O. MacGregor, Mrs J. McInnes, Jack McKay, John McLaren, Donald J. MacLennan, Alastair MacLeod, I. F. McLullich, Mrs M. McNair, Duncan McNeill, D. McNie, A. W. McRobb, Mrs Mary Mann, John C. Marr, Fred Middleton, Mrs J. Millar, R. J. Millar, Mrs Elizabeth Mills, Mrs Kathleen Mills, Miss L. Mitchell, Dr James Morgan, William D. Munro, George Philp, Robin H. Pirie, J. & C. Pocock, Alexander Reiach, Mrs Jean Richardson, Mrs C. Riddell, Mrs Catherine Robertson, D. A. Robertson, Dr H. L. Robertson, Hugh Roy, Maurice Russell, J. A. Sherriff, E. Simpson, J. L. Simpson, Drew Smith, Mrs M. H. Sproule, N. A. R. Stanbra, Mrs A. Stancer, S. W. Stevens-Stratton, the Reverend James Stirling, Minister of St Ninians, Mrs Margaret Strachan, Mrs Margaret Sutherland, Mrs C. M. Swarbrick, "Dod" Suttie, Robert Thomson, William Watson, John White, Mrs A. L.

Williams, James Wilson, John Wilson, Mrs M. Winram, Mrs E. M. Wood, Sir John Wordie, CBE, George T. Wordie, Peter J. Wordie, CBE, James G. Wylie, Cyril Yeoman, Ann Sweeney who did the typing, Robert W. Malster of Terence Dalton Ltd, who has courageously guided publication, and Paul Malster, who gave much assistance with laying out the book.

Most sincere thanks to the following institutions and their staff for their ready and courteous assistance, for finding the answers to countless questions and for going to great lengths to do this:

City of Aberdeen, Libraries Department; Aberdeen University Library; Beamish Museum, Co. Durham, John Gall, Keeper of Development and Rural Life; Belfast, Linen Hall Library; Belfast, Public Library; Belfast, Ulster Museum; Biggar Museum Trust, Albion Archives, Brian Lambie; James Burrough Distillers PLC; Business Archives Council; Clackmannan District Libraries, Alloa; John Dewar & Sons Ltd; Driver and Vehicle Licensing Centre, Swansea; City of Dublin Libraries; City of Dundee District, Public Libraries; City of Edinburgh District Council, Library Services; Falkirk District Council, Public Library; Flair Photographics, Clevedon; the Rector, Glasgow Academy; City of Glasgow District Council, Libraries Department; Glasgow Museum of Transport; Halifax, National Museum of the Working Horse; Inverness, Highland Regional Council, Regional Library Service; Leyland, British Commercial Vehicle Museum; National Motor Museum at Beaulieu, BP Library of Motoring; City of Newcastle-upon-Tyne, Central Library; Northern Ireland, the Public Record Office; Ordnance Survey; Perth and Kinross District Council, District Libraries; Road Haulage Association, Scottish District, Glasgow; Scottish Record Office; Stirling, Archivist of the Central Region Archives, George Dickson; Stirling, District Council Library, Alan Jeffries; Stirling, Smith Art Gallery and Museum, Deborah Haase; Stirling University; Strathclyde Regional Archives, Principal Archivist and staff; Transport and General Workers' Union, Glasgow; United Distillers PLC; University of Glasgow, Dr Sarah C. Orr; Wells Library, Somerset Library Services; Wells, St Andrew's Press.

The Carter's Day 1

IT WAS 5.30 in the morning, a spring morning but blustery because it was still March: Wednesday 29th March, 1939. It was cold too, for spring comes late in Aberdeenshire. I, Raymond Eddie, lived in Fraserburgh, the fishing port on the north-eastern tip of the county, open to north-easterly gales and blizzards straight from Russia. We were in Gallowhill Road up from the harbour and I was fourteen years old, just finished with school.

My family ran a cartage business in the town founded round about 1845 by my great grandfather, William Eddie, and continued by his son, my grandfather James Eddie. His brother, my great-uncle Samuel Eddie, also had a cartage business and my uncle, Arthur Eddie, another, but James Eddie's was the biggest, with fifteen horses stabled in Hanover Street. At fourteen I was too young to join the business; a better plan was to learn cartage in someone else's employ and come back when I was older. I went first to William French, but stayed only a few weeks. I could have tried Gibbs' of Barrisgate Road, but no cartage firm was more respected in Fraserburgh than Wordie & Co. They had been here since the eighteen-seventies; since, indeed, they won a cartage contract with the Great North of Scotland Railway in 1869.

They worked in and out of most of the stations on this system, a railway which had become a model of efficiency. Since 1923 it had been a member of the London & North Eastern group, although we in Fraserburgh still thought of it as the Great North; nothing much changed. Wordie & Co. continued to serve the LNER, although in 1932 there appeared a new title, Wordie's (North Eastern) Ltd, because Wordie & Co. themselves were now closely linked with the rival London, Midland & Scottish group. The new subsidiary remained under the direct control of the family, doing all the old Great North of Scotland work outside Aberdeen. None of this meant anything to me; as far as Fraserburgh was concerned it was still the same old Wordie & Co., although the horse lorries carried the new title along their sides, with LNER at front and rear.

I had been with them only a few weeks, and getting up at five in the morning had been no joke when I started with them in January. But we had to be at the stables in High Street at six, so here I was on my way with my tea can and "piece" for dinner. It was a mile walk down from the house but I made it in time; Bob Connan the foreman was there already and ready to chase

Opposite page: *Horse transport served the fishing industry as well as the railways. A scene at Fraserburgh about 1898 as a cartload of herring nets is brought back from the netstores after tanning.*
George A. Dey

1

Fraserburgh High Street showing the entrance to Wordie's stables at right. Broad Street and the drinking trough for horses is just around the corner off the left-hand side of the picture.
George A. Dey

Below: *The meal kist, lined with metal to keep the rats out. The lids were metal lined, too, and would not stay open, a further anti-rat device.*

E. W. P-T.

latecomers. He lived nearby in Manse Street. It was the custom for foremen to live close to the depot, "on the job".

The Wordie stables were one-storey buildings round three sides of a yard, with the stalls on the long side across the back of the yard. There were eight of them, all occupied in my time. Down one side were a couple of loose boxes for sick horses and the feed store with its kists, or meal bins, metal lined to discourage the rats. Opposite was the shed where the sawdust litter was kept. I forgot to mention the treacle barrel in the feed store, while in one corner of the yard was the water trough and in another the heap of manure, cleared weekly by a local farmer. He generally came on a Saturday morning. Sometimes we had to shift it and dump it, because sawdust does not make very good dung and the farmer did not trouble to come for it.

There were eight of us carters, Alec Dempster, Eric Cardno, Hugh Davidson, "Cripple" Sim, Andrew Lovie, George Watson, Simon Burnett and myself, by far the youngest. My horse was a black Clydesdale mare called Darkie, seven years old, patient and willing. In the early light we turned to to muck out, feed and groom our beasts. There was no stableman, so we did everything. We shovelled up and barrowed out the dung and soiled litter. Then we filled our feed boxes from the corn kists and sacks of chopped hay. These boxes were ten inches by nine inches by nine inches, and when filled held one feed for the horse. They were carried to and emptied into the mangers in each stall morning and evening, and at midday if the horse came back to the stables for his dinner. Otherwise the midday feed was emptied into a feed sack for the nosebag at the station.

The feed was a mixture of chopped hay, cut into inch or so lengths, a little kibbled or broken or crushed maize, and oats, bruised to break the husk, which helped the horse to chew. We gave our horses fourteen pounds of hay each a day, twelve pounds of oats each and two of maize. This added up to twenty-eight pounds, but we generally gave a bit more, say thirty, divided into three feeds, in the morning, less at dinner time, but more at night. All the feed came by train from Aberdeen, where it was prepared in the provender mill at the big Rodger's Walk stables. This had the machinery to cut the hay and bruise the oats. All the smaller depots in the North-east were supplied from Aberdeen; rail was the only way to distribute it before the motor lorry, and it remained the most convenient, for the depots were all near the station. Moreover a motor would have had an empty run back. The sawdust litter came by rail too, in sacks. We never used straw because of the rats it harboured; even so there were plenty of them, but Alec Dempster had a terrier which he left in the yard overnight now and again—there were always a few corpses in the morning.

Along with the feed I gave Darkie a pail of water, and as she ate and drank I groomed her. This was a matter of brushing with the dandy brush, the wooden-backed brush with the leather strap to stop the hand slipping. She had had a lie down during the night and her left side was covered in sawdust. I brushed all this off, working back from the neck, turning then to the right hand or off side, always brushing with the run of the hair. She had lain a bit on this side, too; horses do not settle on one side like a dog, in fact much of the night they are standing up. I paid particular attention to the featherings on her legs, not so much as an English Shire would have. There was always the risk of cuts on the legs; if they were dirty they would become infected. I wiped her over with some sacking and finished off with a good clean of the soles of the feet, making sure the shoes were firm. I had done it all the night before, but we had to be sure before the day's work. Finally I had a good look at Darkie's backside, washing clear all urine stains and wiping off any streaks of dung. She would be more comfortable now.

Darkie's harness or gears hung on two pegs, one at the back of the stall for the collar, hames and breechings, the other on the stall post for the bridle. In the next stall to the right was Danny, Alec Dempster's horse, while to the left was Hugh Davidson's Jock. The harness was hung up as it came off and would go on in the reverse order. I would give it a brush, and if there was time put some boot polish on the leather and Brasso on the metal. Once the harness

E.W.P-T.

3

E·W·P·T

was clean it was not too difficult to keep clean; I would take bits of it home and have a field day on it when I was "toun keeper". This was when I took my turn to look after the horses at the weekend, Saturday afternoons and Sundays. As there were eight of us I was on duty every eighth week. My harness was marvellous that Monday morning, shining leather, buckles and hames winking in the sunlight, chains burnished, done by swinging them in a sack of sawdust mixed with oil and paraffin.

For the heavier four-wheel lorries and for the box carts we used heavy harness, that is the peaked Glasgow collar with the high spreading hames, the peaked Glasgow saddle with two rings for the reins, the back chain passing over the saddle to the shafts, the breeching chain securing the breechings to the shafts so that the horse could check and back the vehicle. For the lighter four-wheel lorries we had the light harness, a non-peaked collar and a light saddle. Through the ridge of this went a leather shaft strap with a loop at each end for the shafts to pass through, while the breechings were secured to the shafts by leather straps. It was an offence to use light harness on a heavy vehicle and the carter could face prosecution. This was a day for heavy harness.

Darkie remained with her halter on while being harnessed. The halter rope was led through a ring on the manger and had a wooden ball attached to its other end. Only when the collar and bridle were put on was the halter taken off and left at the stall. But the first job standing on Darkie's near side was to lay the saddle gently on her broad back, securing the girth and laying the crupper strap out towards the tail, the latter being passed through the dock, the loop at the end. It had been Wordie practice to dock tails, a fashion, but by 1939 they were being left to swish away flies or maybe tied up and plaited. The breechings now fell into place round her stern: a leather band some three inches wide held by loin and hip straps from the crupper.

Now, with Darkie still facing into her stall, the halter was taken off and the collar put on, upside down, and turned gently to the right until the peak came uppermost, the mane being tidied and smoothed down. Round the groove in the collar went the tall out-curving hames, held at the top by the hame strap; and then I fitted the bridle, a closed one in this case, although open ones were used, without blinkers or blinds as we sometimes called them in Scotland. I was careful with the bridle, putting the bit in first and passing the rest over Darkie's head. The bit was a simple snaffle which worked in the corner of the mouth, having a strap and buckle at each end for attachment to the bridle. I removed it when Darkie ate or drank. The reins were led from the bit through the rings on the hames and on the saddle, where they were looped and knotted until needed.

Above: *To keep the horse tied up in the stall, yet free to move without tripping or becoming entangled, the six-foot halter was secured by a wooden weight, called in Ulster a sinker. It was made of lignum vitae three and a half inches in diameter by two and three-quarter inches deep.*

By this time it was getting on for seven; we had to be at the station for half past to pick up our lorries, our orders and our loads. We all trooped out into the yard and gave our beasts another drink at the yard trough. We took with us a nosebag, a sack of feed for dinner, a pail and the Wordie quarter cloth, woven in red and black checks like a tartan with WORDIE'S (NORTH EASTERN) LTD stencilled across it in large white letters. These cloths were to keep the horse warm while standing. Railway work was notorious for delay, waiting for trains, waiting to come up to the right wagon, waiting one's turn at that wagon. It was not so bad at Fraserburgh, a small place, but we heard about the congestion at Waterloo goods station in Aberdeen. Sometimes lorries would be waiting there a couple of hours.

We all had our tough leather aprons, our breeches and gaiters (generally corduroy or serge breeches and leather gaiters), a thick old serge coat and boots stuffed with straw for warmth. Some men had dungarees and a sou'wester but most of us could only afford a cap, while one or two at some places improvised aprons out of bleached seed sacks. Our wages in 1939 were thirty-five shillings

Two trace horses at Maud Junction, where they were needed to help lorries up the local hills.
Alex Reiach

Below: *Broad Street, Fraserburgh, at the beginning of this century. In the background a horse and lorry stands at the drinking trough, and coming up the street is another horse lorry laden with herring barrels.*
George A. Dey

(£1.75) a week, with twopence an hour overtime for the younger carters and sixpence an hour for the older. In modern terms £1.75 is a ludicrous sum, but in 1939, with bread at fourpence (2p) a standard loaf, its purchasing power was reasonable. We all carried a short whip with a two-foot handle and a lash about three feet long. It was pushed in a pocket of the apron, and rarely left it.

Through the town we went in procession, the shoes striking the tarmac (there were no granite cassies here), our own iron-shod boots providing an accompaniment. A few people were about, a milk float, two postmen, shopkeepers taking down their shutters and a policeman yawning at a corner. Alec Dempster led us; he was the senior carter. Before we reached the station in Shore Street, half a mile from our High Street stables, we stopped at the Temperance Fountain in Broad Street to give the horses a final drink before work. Once in the goods yard we backed up to our lorries, which were lined up in front of the goods shed, while Bob Connan, our foreman, opened up the little Wordie office in the yard. We put our folded quarter cloths on the lorry and hung nosebag, feed sack and pail underneath. Once we had backed up we lowered the shafts, guiding the back chains into the bridges of the saddles, which were kept well oiled. Equally well oiled were the slide rods on the shafts, for the chains slid from side to side and

back as the horse moved. Once Darkie felt the weight of the shafts, stopped from riding up by the belly band, she stood quiet as I hooked the drachts or draught chains to the shafts and secured the breechings chains. The reins were untied and laid back to the lorry platform and we were ready to go, except for one thing. Darkie wore a leather muzzle because she had the habit of giving passers-by a quick nip. Since she spent most of the day standing outside shops this could be quite a hazard for the people of Fraserburgh. There was no need to tether our horses when delivering. They stood quietly and moved when ordered.

At the goods station.

It was now half past seven and time we were in the goods station. A train had come in at seven that morning, but there had been a train the evening before so there was a pile of parcels waiting for us, as well as a load of flour for the Co-op, several casks of beer for the pubs and some large items like easy chairs and sofas, a lawnmower, garden tools and a new bacon slicer, a ponderous thing in a packing case, for one of the grocers. Our heavier lorries could carry a ton or more, the lighter not more than ten hundred-weight. The heavier lorry platforms were twelve feet long by five feet wide, surrounded by a choke rail painted reddish brown and lettered on the sides WORDIE'S (NORTH EASTERN) LTD in gold, shaded a deeper gold, with L.N.E.R. similarly executed at front and rear. The iron-tyred wheels were red, as were the underframe, axles, forecarriage and shafts. Each lorry was numbered. We generally kept the same lorry and we were responsible for its maintenance, which was mainly greasing the wheel hubs and the turning table on the forecarriage. This last was important, because a freely swivelling forecarriage made lighter work for the horse. Any repairs or retyring were put out either to Henderson the cartwright or Lippe the blacksmith, who did the Wordie horse shoeing in Fraserburgh.

The goods station at Fraserburgh had four gates, so it was no problem to back up to the loading bank served by a single railway track. The bank, the track and the road approach were so aligned that the level was constant from the floor of the railway wagon to the platform of the horse lorry, no lifting needed. The goods clerk issued our delivery notes from his little office. I was on a parcels round and backed the lorry up to the bank, easier than backing out loaded; indeed, the space forced us to back up for loading. For the young carter backing was something that had to be learned; you had to remember to steer opposite to the intended course. It was no good being impatient with a horse. Although Hugh Davidson's Jock was a bit restive, we were all backed up in a few minutes. Scenes in Glasgow, Belfast and Edinburgh, where Wordie horses were numbered in hundreds, were livelier; thank heavens we were only eight in Fraserburgh.

Parcels are generally bulky rather than heavy, and it took only three-quarters of an hour to load me up. Helped by a porter, I put on a roll of tweed for Maitland's, the outfitters in Cross Street; also for them a carton of those fashionable cloche hats and some rolls of linoleum, as they were also in the furnishing business. For McDonald's the grocers, likewise in Cross Street, I had three cases of tinned fruit, two sacks of oatmeal, a side of bacon, a huge cheese in muslin and a chest of tea. Tindall's the ironmongers were in Cross Street too, and for them I had three bags of nails, two spades and the lawnmower. For McConachie's the fish canners I had a box of labels for their tins. It would take me a couple of hours to deliver all this as, although the shops were close together, the fish cannery was half a mile away in Bath Street, near the harbour. I collected my delivery notes from the clerk and set out.

Driving the lorry was a quiet business, with no shouted words of command; a click of the tongue to start, a pull on the reins for turning left or right, a pull back on both reins and a muttered "whoa" to stop. Signalling to turn was done with the whip held out for right and left. Maybe I would have to shift my seat to signal right, for we generally sat on the nearside on the folded lorry cover, if it was not in use. The springing was harsh. For downhill work the lorry had steel-shod brake blocks on the back wheels, applied by a handwheel turning a worm and nut gear. If it was very steep there was the skidpan or shoe drag, hung by a chain, which could be dropped to lock one of the rear wheels, turning it into a sledge.

I was back at the station by half past ten, having nothing to collect, and handed my sheaf of delivery notes all signed to Bob Connan, who would send them off to Wordie & Co. at Aberdeen for invoicing to the railway. The LNER goods clerk now wanted me to take twenty sacks of flour, each weighing a hundredweight, to the Co-op bakery. This made two loads and was checked on the

E.W. PAGET-TOMLINSON.

weighbridge, as charges for railway work went by weight unless they were "smalls", under one hundredweight, or parcels as I had just had. It would take me until midday to deliver the flour and come back for dinner, for the Co-op bakery was in High Street, about a mile away. I saw that someone else had taken the bacon slicer, which pleased me, and that the beer had gone. This would mean a drink at every pub for the lucky carter; we would know who it was at dinner time; probably Dempster, who liked his half-and-half and generally managed to secure the liquid deliveries. I was too young, anyway.

It was still cold and windy as Darkie and I set out once more into more crowded streets, with motors and shoppers all over the place. Because of the flour I was thankful it was not raining, but I did spread my cover in case the wind brought a shower off the sea. Ten sacks per load made a single tier, so it was easy to run out the cover and spread it sideways. Each side had ties which could be secured to the hooks along the sides of the platform, of which there were five, one on each end of each cross bearer under the platform. At the bakery I had to carry the hundredweight flour sacks to the store myself, tough work for a fourteen year old; fortunately it was on the ground floor.

When I came back at dinner time I found all the others there and the horses tied up in a patient row with their nosebags. Darkie went to the end and I filled her bag from the feed sack. Then I took her pail to the yard tap. The men brewed their tea and ate their "pieces" in the porters' room behind the goods station. I saw now who had been on the pub round; I was right, it was Alec Dempster.

The morning's work had cleared the bank, but another train came in at half past one and there was as much work again for the afternoon. I loaded more parcels for the shops, sacks of sugar for the grocer's, saucepans for the ironmonger and boxes of shoes from Street in Somerset as well as sole leather for the two shoe repairers in Batchensbrae, Colvin's and Dunn's; and for Claud Alexander a bolt of tartan, appropriately the Clan Gordon. Hamilton's the solicitors in Broad Street took two boxes of stationery off me, while there were a few parcels for private houses in Grattan Place and in Saltoun Place. One looked like a standard lamp, another box felt like a safe. I had to collect some parcels from this part of the town for the evening train to Aberdeen.

Batchensbrae, Fraserburgh, where Raymond Eddie delivered sole leather for the shoe repairers. The correct name of this thoroughfare is Frithside Street; it acquired its popular name from the ship chandlery and ironmonger's shop of Mr Batchen on the right-hand side of this picture.
George A. Dey

I had finished by about five and went back to the station with my parcels and delivery notes for Bob Connan, and unyoked. We backed the lorries in against the wall, lifted the shafts and led the horses out. The return to the stables was a cheerful procession; the horses would nearly do the Highland Fling. On the way we stopped again at the Temperance Fountain for a drink, but on arrival at the High Street the animals went straight to their stalls. Unharnessing was quickly accomplished: breechings and saddle, bridle and collar,

the latter turned upside down again to lift it gently over the ears and down past the face. Once the harness was hung up, Darkie, now with her halter on, was tethered and awaited her feed. This was the same as in the morning, although once a week treacle was added, and occasionally a chopped turnip. We gave a bran mash now and again as a tonic, and linseed soaked and boiled as a laxative and conditioner; this improved the coat. While Darkie fed I groomed her again, paying particular attention to her feet after her day on the streets. I also put down fresh sawdust.

By about six we were done and we went home, Bob Connan locking the yard gate. He had left his office at the station during the day to see to a load of feed which one of the lorries had brought off the train and had also been to see William Lippe, the horseshoer, to arrange for two of the horses to be shod; they might wear a set of shoes out in a couple of weeks on the streets. His last task had been to send off the day's delivery notes and weight tickets to the Wordie office in Aberdeen by the half past five train for the clerks there to make up the railway accounts.

Evening chores.

Living near in Manse Street, Bob Connan could keep an eye on the horses. He was on call night and day seven days a week, some responsibility. In winter we had paraffin lamps to light when we came in, but it was spring now. Sometimes we did work late, when a ship had to be unloaded. If it was a coal cargo the box carts were put to work. They could carry up to fifteen hundredweights at a time and each might make eight trips a day between the ship and the gasworks and the local coal merchants. We had four of these carts, so altogether they would handle about 24 tons a day; clearing a coaster with a capacity of two to three hundred tons was a slow job. Other cartage firms were generally involved, the late working coming when the ship had to catch the night tide.

Another import was for the herring fishing, barrel staves from Denmark and Sweden, each two feet six inches long. One horse lorry could manage about eight or nine loads of staves a day from the harbour to the coopers. Both the lorries and the box carts were helped up from the harbour by trace horses, needed particularly for loads of logs.

A special occasion was Lifeboat Day, when Alec Dempster turned out with a pair to parade the boat through the town. He needed tracers, so the rest of the stable came to help. Then there were the herring landings, which kept Wordie's busy from June to September with extra horses, lorries and men sent up from Aberdeen.

So ends a Wordie day, not a typical one because no day was ever typical; a Wordie day in a small stables in north-east Scotland about the same size as the stables in Stirling, where and when the business started.

Early Days 2

COMMUNICATIONS were not good in Central Scotland in the eighteenth century. Up to 1709 the mail between Edinburgh and Glasgow was carried on foot; thereafter the post boy had a pony. Then in 1747 the Edinburgh & Glasgow Caravan Company started a twice-weekly stage coach service which by 1765 had become daily, taking nine hours for the fifty-odd miles. Parallel with the passenger vehicles were stage waggons, not running to fixed timetables as the coaches did, and many carts on local carrying work. Tonnages were low because of the limitations of roads and vehicles, although legislation sought to improve conditions. At the same time demands were growing, notably for coal, needed not only by industry but by everyone for keeping warm and cooking.

English colliery owners had built canals to transport their coal, and the proprietors of the pits in Lanarkshire followed their example. By 1773 a canal had been opened from the Monklands district for about nine and a half miles to the north-eastern outskirts of Glasgow, but it stopped short for lack of funds. Nine years later work restarted on the section of canal into Glasgow and in 1790 on an extension eastwards to tap water from the Calder, the whole 12¼-mile system being completed by 1793, three years after the full opening of Scotland's most important waterway, the Forth & Clyde Canal; work on this had been started in 1768, two years before the Monkland.

This coast-to-coast route had been considered as early as the reign of Charles II to solve Central Scotland's transport, but the scheme had to wait over a century before being brought to fruition. Its engineer, John Smeaton, replanned it as a ship canal, which much improved its potential. It was open from the Forth to a terminal basin in Glasgow by 1778, but there was no money to continue westwards to the Clyde. However, the government came to the rescue and in 1790 the canal reached the Clyde at Bowling, where the river was deeper. Ships could use the canal from Glasgow to reach east coast ports, including London, and the Continent, while from the improved Glasgow terminal, Port Dundas, the "cut of junction" was made to meet the Monkland. Finally and much later came the Edinburgh & Glasgow Union Canal, which ran from the Forth & Clyde near Falkirk 31½ miles into Edinburgh. Begun in 1817 and opened in 1822, this was not a ship canal but was built on the English model with fixed bridges.

Opposite page:
William Wordie (1810–1874), who saw the railways not as competitors to the road carrier but as a source of business. He made a contract with the Edinburgh & Glasgow Railway in 1842 to collect and forward goods, thus laying the foundations of Wordie & Co. P. J. Wordie

Nevertheless it was successful in bringing coal to Edinburgh, and like the Forth & Clyde became busy with passenger boats, although the latter derived increasing revenue from expanding mineral traffic to the newly built foundries.

The Monkland Canal inspired railway building, seen in the early nineteenth century as a means of feeding a canal. Generally these horse-worked lines came down to the canal, but by the eighteen-twenties the Monkland was carrying all the traffic its water supply could manage. Moreover, for eastwards traffic it faced the wrong way. To bring Lanarkshire coal to Edinburgh a new more direct route was needed, best served by a railway. But it was still a waterway-dominated railway, since it ran from the coalfield down to the Forth & Clyde at Kirkintilloch. Opened in 1826, it was at first horse worked, but in 1831 the first steam locomotive was put to use. This was the year of opening of the Garnkirk & Glasgow, notable on two counts, apart from the emphasis on Garnkirk, a mining community east of Glasgow. It was the first railway in Scotland to be promoted independently of a canal and the first to use steam locomotives from the start. It was needed for the same reason as the canals and their railway feeders, to bring coal, this time to Tennants' chemical works at St Rollox by the canal basins in Glasgow, for the Tennants found the canal could not bring them sufficient fuel. The railway's Glasgow terminus was Townhead, the first passenger station in the city; this was a line which carried people as well as minerals.

To road carriers waterways were competitive in the sense that they offered another form of transport, but a water route was inflexible, a main line with few branches. Canals suffered acutely from difficulties in the collection and distribution of goods, a problem which was also to plague the later railways. The Monkland had four short branches serving collieries and iron works, the Forth & Clyde the long Glasgow branch, a limeworks branch near Castlecary and side cuts into the Carron and the Clyde opposite the entrance to the Cart, the Union no branches. No canal networks like the Birmingham system developed in Scotland, so road carriers were free to come and go between wharf, warehouse, mill, shop and dwelling. Moreover the Scottish canals, particularly the Monkland, concentrated on bulk cargoes, for which boats were better suited than road waggons. The latter could be more profitably employed on high-toll goods, bales of cloth, liquids in cask, produce, parcels.

There was one attempt to marry rail, road and water. In about 1835 a coal waggon boat was put on the Forth & Clyde to carry waggons off the Monkland & Kirkintilloch Railway, an early train ferry with rails and a turntable, and it proved profitable. There was a similar coal-cart boat, an early roll-on, roll-off ferry, which could

E.W. PAGET-TOMLINSON

Roll-on, roll-off transport is no new idea: in 1833 the Forth & Clyde Canal experimented with an iron scow carrying eighteen carts on deck. Two years later tramroad waggon scows carrying fourteen waggons loaded with a total of forty tons of coal were tried with success.

carry eighteen carts, while the waggon boat could carry fourteen waggons.

Horse-worked railways were likewise competitive to roads, but again their route was inflexible and linked with the traffic of the canal they generally served, bulk cargoes predominating. With the steam locomotive, however, came a serious threat to the road carrier. That threat came not from the early steam locomotive confined to colliery lines, the "Puffing Billy" type, but from the advanced machine which the Stephensons demonstrated at Rainhill in 1830, the *Rocket*, capable of sustained fast running and able to draw a considerable load compared with a horse and cart.

By 1830 there were many railway schemes afoot in Scotland, but they waited to see how the Garnkirk & Glasgow would turn out. Once it was opened in 1831 its success encouraged further promotion of many other railways, not least of lines between the two principal cities, Glasgow and Edinburgh. Eventually in 1838 a company called the Edinburgh & Glasgow Railway secured an Act for a line which would closely parallel the Forth & Clyde and Union Canals and cream off their passenger and light goods traffic, but probably not their mineral trade. At the same time it would capture anything which was going long-distance on the roads.

Engineered as a high-speed line save for the descent to the new Glasgow terminus in Queen Street, which became an operational nightmare, the Edinburgh & Glasgow was opened on 21st February, 1842. Four trains daily were advertised each way, taking between two and a quarter and two and half hours for the fifty-mile journey, although an early-morning third class and luggage train took longer. All the road passenger coaches could offer was a four-hour journey with, they said, more personal attention; this was at least an advance, because of the improved roads, on the nine hours of the mid-eighteenth century. Both coaches and canal passenger boats were hit, inter-city passenger

15

traffic by canal ceasing by 1848, although short-distance services were run for a decade or two. For William Wordie, a road carrier between Stirling and Glasgow, the building of a goods station at the railway's Queen Street terminus posed a threat to his business.

William Wordie was born in 1810, the son of John Wordie, who married Janet Stewart and ran a road carrier's business in the Stirling area. There had been Wordies at Torbrex and Cambusbarron near Stirling since the late fifteenth century. The name might then have been Worthy, but whatever it was there seem to have been plenty of them in succeeding centuries. A sixteenth-century Thomas Wordye was a friar at Cambuskenneth Abbey, a seventeenth-century John Wordie of Torbrex a minister of religion in Stirling, while in 1685 William Wordie of Cambusbarron gave a silver Communion cup to the Church of St Ninians near Stirling.

By the eighteenth century both the Torbrex and Cambusbarron Wordies were farmers and property owners of some substance. One of them had in 1682 completed the building of Williamsfield House at St Ninians, a considerable property which still stands. Two eighteenth-century Wordie brothers sought fortunes in India, one dying in the service of the East India Company at Calcutta at the age of twenty-five, while the other, yet another William, who had been an Edinburgh merchant, likewise went to Calcutta to recoup his finances and died there in 1787. He

So far this scrap of a bill dated 1818 is the earliest evidence of Wordie cartage revenue. John Wordie was paid 12s 7d freight charges from Liverpool, presumably by sea, and cartage from Glasgow, most likely to Stirling. P. J. Wordie is remembered to this day for his bequest of money whose interest is even now distributed each year to the poor of St Ninians, what in Scotland is called a mortification. Evidence of the family's property ownership can still be seen, the "W" initials which mark many houses in St Ninians to this day.

Stirling Castle.

More relevant to cartage is the mid-eighteenth-century Thomas Wordie, clerk to the Incorporated Society of Carters of Stirling, who wrote a minute, now preserved at the Smith Institute there, describing the arrival of Prince Charles Edward in the Royal Burgh in 1745. Thomas was not a Jacobite, although most of the Wordies were; if they were not, they married Jacobites. One of them, indeed, is believed to have entertained the Prince during his stay in Stirling.

So there is some evidence of Wordie cartage at this date, a natural extension of the activities of a farmer with his horse and cart. If cartage proved profitable he would be likely to undertake more work, and this must have happened because John Wordie, born in 1783 or 1784, the son of James Wordie who died in 1793, was established as a road carrier in the early nineteenth century. He it was who ran an illegal mail service from Stirling to Glasgow, Edinburgh and London between 1807 and 1825, charging sixpence halfpenny (3p) to Glasgow, eightpence (between 3p and 4p) to Edinburgh and one shilling and twopence (6p) to London. He was in no position to carry letters to London; most probably he put them aboard the Leith packet, quite unofficially, for she would be carrying the Post Office mails. There is no doubt about his operations in the eighteen-twenties, which appear in *Pigot's Commercial Directory for Scotland*, when he ran from Bannockburn to Glasgow on Mondays and Thursdays, while in 1829 an entry appears for the first time in the Glasgow Post Office Directory giving him an address, 35 Blackfriars Street in Glasgow. This would have been somewhere for him to receive goods for carriage back to Stirling and to store goods for collection.

It is supposed that John Wordie's business did not prosper, because by the late eighteen-twenties he became financially embarrassed. He died suddenly in 1830 when out for his Sunday walk, leaving half a dozen horses and a few carts for his son William, then twenty, to carry on as best he could. William was a man of energy and rapidly paid off his father's creditors. In a few years he was able to offer better carriage between Stirling and Glasgow, certainly from 1837 when his carts ran daily from Bannockburn and from Stirling itself to Glasgow; possibly the same cart starting from his warehouse in Dumbarton Road, Stirling, called at Bannockburn—which remained a depot until 1948. William Wordie's Stirling office was in May Day Yard, but he had agents in other parts of the town who would receive goods for him.

In 1837 he took a partner, John McArthur; the partnership lasted only until 1841. On 20th December, 1837, he married Janet, daughter of Peter Jeffrey of Throsk on the Forth below Stirling. The latter, who died in 1842, was a well-to-do farmer and landowner who held an interest in the Alloa ferry, of which William Wordie made considerable use. Of Peter Jeffrey's other daughters, one, Anne, married John McEwan of the brewing dynasty; her daughter in turn married into another brewing family, the Youngers, who later became distinguished in other fields. A sampler worked by Janet Jeffrey survives.

By this time the railway age was fast approaching Scotland: the Edinburgh & Glasgow, Scotland's first main-line railway, secured their Act in 1838. William Wordie and a few others realized that the railway could bring them business. Their perception was acute, for in the eighteen-thirties no one could know how the railway would affect other methods of transport. There were few railways from which to judge: the Liverpool & Manchester had been completed in 1830; the Grand Junction from the Liverpool &

Early railways in Central Scotland. The map shows clearly the mineral lines feeding the canals as well as the first line into Glasgow, the Garnkirk & Glasgow, opened in 1831, and the first Scottish inter-city line, the Edinburgh & Glasgow, opened in 1842. This was the railway whose cartage work William Wordie secured, beginning his career as a railway carrier.

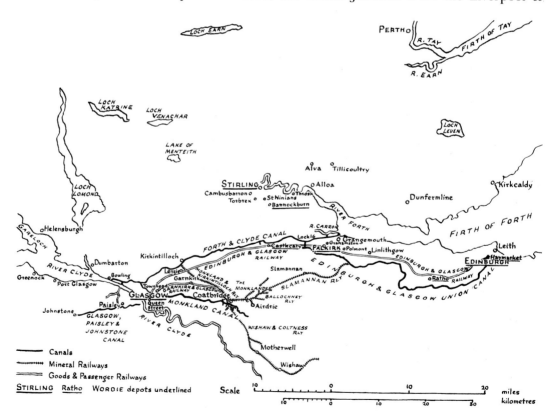

A contemporary print of the opening of the Garnkirk & Glasgow Railway in 1831, from a drawing by David Octavius Hill.

Manchester to Birmingham opened in 1837; the London & Birmingham in 1838.

Whether William Wordie actually saw these railways at this early date is not known, but they were not then regarded as great goods carriers. Indeed the early railway companies neither saw themselves as nor acted as carriers. They followed the river and canal tradition by providing a road on which others could run on payment of a toll. It was thought at first that the carriers would steam their own trains as they navigated their boats, but this was quickly seen to create operational difficulties and the railway companies had to provide the motive power and run the trains. But these could be made up of private wagons, a tradition that persisted until nationalization and is revived today, as indeed is the prospect of private trains competing for business on a track provided by another authority to whom tolls would be paid.

In the early railway days the goods in these wagons were handled and forwarded by the contractors who owned them, among whom were Pickford's, who entered the railway scene from the roads and canals. But this method whereby contractors handled the full transit of goods from collection to delivery, involving both road and rail transport, did not last. The railways came to organize their own carrying business on their permanent way and increasingly from the eighteen-sixties their own road cartage. Road operations had been allowed them under Acts of 1845 and 1854, but much reliance continued to be placed on agents, and in Scotland, North-east England and South-west England this continued into the twentieth century, which explains the expansion of Wordie & Co. and of their rivals; as the railways grew, they grew.

In 1842, therefore, William Wordie made a contract with the Edinburgh & Glasgow Railway, undertaking to collect and forward goods on the railway. Goods would arrive at the station in his carts, be loaded on his railway wagons and be offloaded into his carts at the other end, so providing a Wordie door-to-door service. For this he opened cartage depots along the line, at Castlecary, Falkirk and Ratho, as well as offices in Edinburgh; or rather he made use of other people's offices, one being on Princes Street, and naturally he was at the Edinburgh terminus of the Edinburgh & Glasgow Railway, then at Haymarket.

He had perceived the railway's need for road cartage to collect and deliver the goods it could so rapidly carry, a need which would grow as the rail network spread. Moreover, the speed and capacity of trains would bring an ever-greater volume of business, although this would have been difficult to forecast in 1842. For him there was every inducement to co-operate; his inherited business was at a low ebb. He could not do much worse but he might do a great deal better.

An advertisement from the Aberdeen Journal *of 11th November, 1854, recording the appointment of Wordie & Co. as sole agents of the Aberdeen Railway Company.* Aberdeen Journals Ltd. and City of Aberdeen Libraries

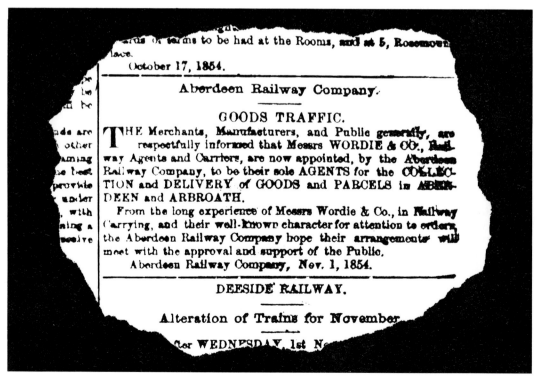

... of terms to be had at the Rooms, and at 5, Rosemount
place.

October 17, 1854.

Aberdeen Railway Company.

GOODS TRAFFIC.

THE Merchants, Manufacturers, and Public generally, are respectfully informed that Messrs WORDIE & CO., Railway Agents and Carriers, are now appointed, by the Aberdeen Railway Company, to be their sole AGENTS for the COLLECTION and DELIVERY of GOODS and PARCELS in ABERDEEN and ARBROATH.

From the long experience of Messrs Wordie & Co., in Railway Carrying, and their well-known character for attention to orders, the Aberdeen Railway Company hope their arrangements will meet with the approval and support of the Public.

Aberdeen Railway Company, Nov. 1, 1854.

DEESIDE RAILWAY.

Alteration of Trains for November

...for WEDNESDAY, 1st N...

Railway Carrier 3

THAT the railways brought increased business and therefore industrialization to Central Scotland was soon evident, for example at Falkirk, where between 1842 and 1877 thirteen new foundries and five new ironworks were built. Falkirk was on the Edinburgh & Glasgow; other centres were to benefit as the railway system spread. Most pushing was the Caledonian, incorporated in 1845 to build a line from Carlisle to Glasgow and Edinburgh but ambitious to expand in other directions. The Carlisle line, which divided at Carstairs to serve Edinburgh and Glasgow, was opened on 15th February, 1848; the Edinburgh terminus was at Lothian Road, while in Glasgow in 1849 a station called South Side was built to the south of the Clyde. It was used for a short while only by trains from the south, which from 1st November, 1849, ran into the new Caledonian terminus, Buchanan Street. Glasgow Central opened much later, in 1879.

On 7th August, 1849, the Caledonian opened a line from their existing system northwards to pass under the Edinburgh & Glasgow at Castlecary and meet the new Scottish Central end on at Greenhill near Falkirk. This last had been authorized in 1845 to push the metals forward to Stirling and Perth. It, too, was completed in 1848, bringing Perth within three hours or so of Glasgow; the old Garnkirk & Glasgow terminus at Townhead was replaced by Buchanan Street, where a goods station opened the following year.

Beyond Perth railway progress was in the hands of the Scottish Midland Junction, which ran from Perth up Strathmore to Coupar Angus and Forfar, the Dundee & Perth, the Dundee & Arbroath (opened as an isolated local line as early as 1838) and the Aberdeen Railway. All these lines were completed by 1850, linking Aberdeen with the South, albeit circuitously, for as yet there were no Forth or Tay bridges. For this reason the Edinburgh & Glasgow were interested in the traffic potential of the Scottish Central, likewise joining up with them at Greenhill and allowing Scottish Central trains to run into Glasgow Queen Street. For the benefit of northwards traffic from Edinburgh the Stirlingshire & Midland Junction had been authorized in 1846 to run from Polmont on the Edinburgh & Glasgow via Grahamston (Falkirk) to join the Scottish Central near Larbert. This line was opened in 1850.

To gain traffic from Alloa and Fife the Scottish Central in 1850 opened a line from north of Larbert to South Alloa on the south side of the Forth whence the ferry, by 1850 steam worked, ran to Alloa. Coal, beer and the woollen products of the Hill Foots, the villages at the foot of the Ochil Hills, Alva and Tillicoultry being the prominent ones, were the principal traffics. Fife coal came in 1850 when the Stirling & Dunfermline Railway reached Alloa from the east, building in 1851 a branch to Tillicoultry and to the ferry berth on the north side.

With Stirling linked to Glasgow by rail and moreover on the only route north, William Wordie's railway association assumed greater importance. It was not enough to have an office at Glasgow's Queen Street station for Edinburgh & Glasgow Railway work. To undertake other railway contracts he needed independence, achieved in 1849 when, again partnered with John McArthur, he opened premises in Argyle Street in Glasgow. This partnership lasted to 1852; thereafter came the historic title Wordie & Co. That year, 1852, is thought to have been when the head office moved from Stirling to Glasgow, to the Argyle Street premises, for William Wordie by then had a house in Glasgow, 148 Renfrew Street. In 1858 he moved first to 175 St Vincent Street, then to a house in Charing Cross, by which time he also had a country house, Garngabber near Lenzie. For his horses in Glasgow he probably went to livery stables, as was the general practice, until stables were rented in Paul Street, Townhead, certainly by 1860; these stables were later bought.

McArthur was sometimes in alliance, sometimes in opposition. When William Wordie and he parted in 1841 McArthur set up his own carrier business between Stirling and Glasgow in association with Archibald Watt. In Glasgow they used premises in Miller's Place off King Street, opposite to where Wordie and McArthur had been based, but after 1852 John McArthur dropped out, although the family continued as carriers in Stirling well into the twentieth century. He was, however, associated with William Wordie in what was afterwards seen to be a momentous step, for in 1851 Wordie, McArthur & Co. were advertised as agents for the Caledonian Railway. They continued to serve the Edinburgh & Glasgow, however, from their Argyle Street office and were indeed back at Queen Street and at the Edinburgh & Glasgow's goods station at Sighthill on the north side of the city in 1855.

But William Wordie's main interest was in the railways with which the Caledonian was by that time linked, notably the Scottish Central and the lines northward. By 1854 he had gained a rail carriage and road cartage contract with the Scottish Central which demanded a new office and depot in Thistle Street in Stirling, near the station. Hitherto he had been working from his warehouse in Dumbarton Road, where his stables remained, and from his old office in May Day Yard. He was also in 1854 a carrier on the

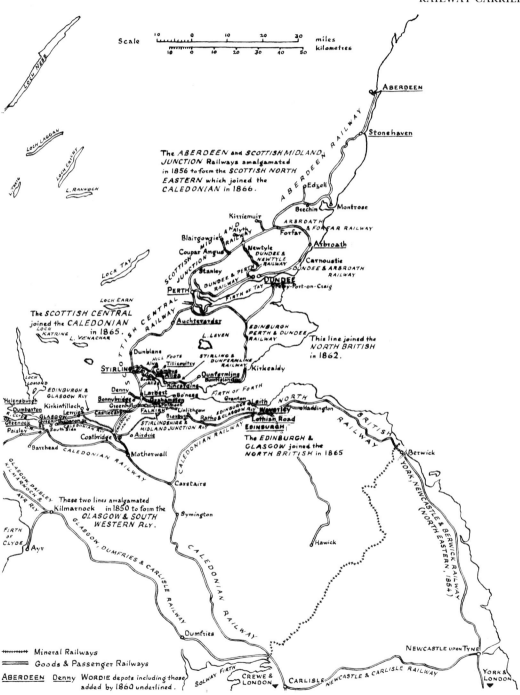

Dundee & Arbroath Railway, which brought business from companies linked with them, the Scottish Midland Junction, the Dundee & Perth and the Aberdeen.

An advertisement in the back of the 1853 Glasgow Post Office Directory describes a working arrangement with the Manchester and London carriers Pickford's, an arrangement which continued throughout Wordie & Co.'s history, latterly with Hay's Wharf, who from 1920 controlled Pickford's. By 1850 the latter were entrenched as carriers on the railway. Through this connection William Wordie, whose company was to be called the "Pickford's of Scotland", could collect goods from Scottish addresses and arrange their carriage to English destinations, the directory listing London, Manchester, Liverpool, Leeds, Hull, Birmingham and Sheffield. At the same time he would deliver in Scotland goods from England consigned by Pickford's.

He had by then an office at Buchanan Street, the Caledonian's Glasgow terminus, and more depots at the stations of the railways with which he had secured contracts. In 1856 he had a depot at Perth as agent for the Scottish Central and the Scottish North Eastern, an amalgamation in July of that year of the Scottish Midland Junction and the Aberdeen railways; in 1856, too, he was at Dundee at Seagate; he had been at Alloa since 1850 and in Aberdeen since 1854. That was the year William Wordie secured his contract with the Aberdeen Railway, and he opened an office in Arbroath at the same time.

An advertisement placed by Wordie & Co. in the *Stirling Observer* for Thursday, 7th April, 1853, makes the scope of the

Sailing vessels in Alloa harbour. One of Wordie & Co.'s early offices was in Alloa, and William Wordie did much to foster traffic by the Alloa ferry across the Forth.

business plain. Because of the Pickford's link and arrangements with other leading carriers the company could offer carriage "to and from all the principal towns and villages of the United Kingdom, Glasgow, Edinburgh, Alloa, Tillicoultry and the Hill Foots trade". As has been explained, William Wordie had done much to foster traffic by the Alloa ferry, in concert with the Scottish Central Railway. However in 1852, the year before this advertisement, the Stirling & Dunfermline Railway had reached Stirling from Alloa and ferry traffic declined. But the Wordie interest did not go unmarked, for in November, 1852, the proprietor of the Ferry Inn at South Alloa gave a supper to Mr and Mrs Wordie and a silver teapot to the latter in recognition of Mr Wordie's work for the Alloa ferry. The silver remains in the family and is a reminder not only of the Wordie but also of the Jeffrey interest in the ferry.

Eventually in 1885 the ferry was replaced by a railway bridge, but Wordie interest in Alloa was maintained, particularly in the beer traffic, for which Wordie's became known. The 1853 advertisement ends with a list of Wordie & Co. offices from which rates information could be gained: Glasgow, Stirling, Alloa, Dundee, Greenock, Perth railway station, Aberdeen station, the Edinburgh & Glasgow Railway office in Edinburgh and from Pickford's in England. A later advertisement, in July, 1853, offers reduced rates to win traffic for the new contracts. The company was expanding.

Surviving ledgers for the period 1856 to 1860 give a detailed insight into the business. Work for the Scottish Central and the Scottish North Eastern figures prominently. By 1860 a depot had been added at Stonehaven and the weekly receipts for cartage for the Scottish North Eastern at Aberdeen and Stonehaven in September, 1860, were between £50 and £60, considerable sums in those days, representing a year's wages for many. Stirling was earning about £80 a week at the same time for railway work, divided into cartage, parcels and haulage, this last the provision of horses and vehicles on hire; linseed, oatmeal and the castings for a gate appear as specific tasks. In spite of the increasingly strong Caledonian connection there was still plenty of work for the Edinburgh & Glasgow, and in 1860 this included parcels deliveries in Stirling, Alloa, nearby Tillicoultry, Kincardine, Dunfermline and Grahamston, which is a part of Falkirk. There was also work at Helensburgh and Dumbarton.

Going back to 1856, an account from Wordie & Co. to the Dundee & Arbroath Railway dated 7th July explains the work in detail: four shillings (20p) a day for the use of a parcel van, two shillings and sixpence (12p) for the hire of a horse. This illustrates how the carrier was paid: the rates for which Wordie's would undertake the work were agreed with the railway, to whom monthly, or maybe in the early days weekly, accounts were

The St Rollox works of the Garnkirk & Glasgow Railway, from a lithograph by David Octavius Hill.

Buchanan Street, Glasgow, in 1911 with a Cowan & Co. lorry prominent in the right foreground. Cowan's were the North British cartage agents and so in opposition to Wordie & Co. From *Glasgow Old and New* by Jack House, 1974, by kind permission of the author.

submitted. Wordie's collected the railway's charges to the customer and passed the money on to the railway company's goods department.

The eighteen-sixties were a decade of railway company amalgamations: 1865 was the great year when the Caledonian gained the Scottish Central and the Edinburgh & Glasgow passed to the North British, the railway which linked Edinburgh with Berwick and the South. Following the Scottish Central, in 1866 the Caledonian took over the Scottish North Eastern, by which means they acquired the line to Aberdeen via Forfar. There were thus two large railways in competition in South and Central Scotland, and William Wordie could not well serve both. He had gained work for what were now satellites of the Caledonian and decided to remain with what became Scotland's largest railway company, a choice which offered prospects of more expansion. Another Edinburgh & Glasgow cartage agent, J. & P. Cameron, also Glasgow based, went on to serve the North British and remained in business until 1926. Like William Wordie they had been early in the field on railway work, agreeing that co-operation was the best policy. They were later to act as agents in Scotland for the English North Eastern and Great Northern railways, and like Wordie & Co. worked for the Great North of Scotland and for the Highland, and indeed for the Caledonian themselves. Cameron's had offices in Buchanan Street, Queen Street and elsewhere in Glasgow.

Wordie's main rivals were Cowan & Co., who had also started in Stirling, but not until the eighteen-fifties. They too became based in Glasgow and grew to be the principal agents for the North British in the city. They also secured work from the Glasgow & South Western and added, as Wordie's did towards the end of the nineteenth century, contracts with shipping companies, in Cowan's case G. & J. Burns' Glasgow to Belfast steamers, the London & Edinburgh Shipping Company, M. Langlands & Sons and, as will be seen in Northern Ireland, the Belfast–Fleetwood steamer cartage in Belfast and the contract for the Belfast & County Down Railway. Then there was the Dundee firm of Mutter Howey who also worked for the North British and established themselves in eastern Scotland from Aberdeen to Berwick and Newcastle, becoming financially associated with the North British Railway and later with the London & North Eastern.

Although well served by Wordie & Co., the Caledonian decided in 1870 to set up its own cartage department, following the practice of the major English companies. Another of their cartage agents was the smaller firm of Charles Robb and Co., headed by Mr George Robb, who was appointed carting superintendent of the Caledonian, bringing his horses and lorries with him; the railway also secured the Caledonian side of J. & P. Cameron's business.

Railway work did not stop Wordie & Co. from continuing to offer a road carrier service between Bannockburn and Glasgow in the eighteen-sixties, "occasionally", says Slater's 1867 directory, which also describes a similar service run by Hill and Cowan, likewise from Bannockburn to Glasgow. Cowan's appear to have continued thus into the eighteen-eighties.

Railway building to the North started from Aberdeen in 1845 when the Great North of Scotland was incorporated to make a line from Aberdeen to Inverness via Elgin and Nairn. This was before railways were complete between Aberdeen and the South. The Great North, however, did not make good progress, and not until 1856 did they reach Keith. To achieve the link with Inverness two further companies were promoted, the Inverness & Nairn, opened in 1855, and the Inverness & Aberdeen Junction, which built on to Keith, reaching there in 1858.

William Wordie was determined to handle the cartage for this new route, a natural extension of his established work at Aberdeen

There is photographic evidence for an eighteen-nineties Wordie's carrier's cart, a two-wheeled vehicle with built-up sides and possibly a canvas cover. The arrangement and style of lettering come from the photograph; the colours are not known; probably red predominated.
David C. Lochrie

27

By 1867 Wordie's were well established as cartage agents to the railways which in 1865 had amalgamated to form the Highland Railway. This timetable, on the front page of the John O'Groat Journal *for 4th April, 1867, shows the extent of the Highland's operations.* P. J. Wordie

for the Scottish North Eastern. By 1860 he had opened a depot in Inverness, with others at Nairn, Forres, Elgin, Fochabers and Keith. They were all small, as the pioneer ones had been in Glasgow and Edinburgh. There were then four horses at Inverness, four at Elgin, one at Nairn and one at Forres, while at Fochabers and Keith a horse was hired locally for the work. At Inverness there were two lorries, one cart and one van; even at Perth in 1860 William Wordie had only two lorries, two parcels vans, four other vans and six carts, while thirteen horses were then sufficient for his work at Stirling.

The business was growing and the new depots in the north established William Wordie in an area of railway development centred on Inverness. Thus by 1864 the Inverness & Ross-shire had reached Bonar Bridge at the head of the Dornoch Firth. In the south a line from Perth to Dunkeld had been opened in 1856, but the major promotion came in 1861: the Inverness & Perth Junction was formed to drive a line from Forres on the Inverness & Aberdeen Junction over the mountains to meet the Perth & Dunkeld, which the bigger company took over when in September, 1863, the new railway was completed. The direct line from Aviemore via Carr Bridge came much later; it was opened in 1898.

It will be remembered that 1865 was the year of Scottish railway amalgamations. Not only did the Scottish Central unite with the Caledonian, and the Edinburgh & Glasgow with the North British, but now the Inverness & Perth and the Inverness & Aberdeen (which had taken over the Inverness & Nairn in 1861) joined up to form the Highland Railway. Railway building west and north of Inverness took longer; Strome Ferry was reached in 1870, the line being extended to the Kyle of Lochalsh in 1897, while Thurso and Wick were linked to Inverness in 1874.

Already established in Inverness and Elgin as cartage agent for the Inverness & Aberdeen Junction Railway, William Wordie became agent for the new Highland Railway in 1868. This move led to the establishment of depots northwards to Bonar Bridge and beyond, at Beauly, Dingwall, Fearn, and right up to Wick and Thurso by 1875. The Dingwall stables seem to have been open by 1871, and those at Invergordon by 1872, while by 1875 stables are recorded at Tain and Fort George. Strictly these northward and westward lines were opened by independent companies, but the Highland worked them from the start, taking over the Dingwall to Skye line in 1880 and the Thurso in 1884. On the Skye line Wordie's had a stable at Achnasheen and eventually a depot at the Kyle.

More extensive was the company's involvement with the Great North of Scotland Railway. After its shaky start this company made better progress, making its own way to Elgin via Craigellachie, with

---

HIGHLAND RAILWAY.

ON 1st MARCH, 1867, and until further notice, the Trains will arrive and depart at the following hours, or as near thereto as circumstances will permit. Time taken from the Railway Clocks.

UP TRAINS.

STATIONS.	1 Parl. Class 1 & 3	2 Pass. Class 1 & 3	3 Mail Class 1 & 3	4 Mxd Class 1 & 3	5 Pass. Class 1 & 3	6 Pass. Class 1 & 3	7 Pass. Class 1 & 3	8 Pass. Class 1 & 3
Coaches leave Thurso,		4 53r						
Wick,		7 28						
Golspie,		3 32a						
Trains Leave		A.M.	A.M.		A.M.			P.M.
Bonar Bridge,		6 50	9 20					4 0
Eiderton,		7 13	9 45					4 20
Meikle Ferry,		7 22	9 55					4 31
Tain,		7 30	10 4		11 40			4 39
Fearn,		7 42	10 14		11 53			4 48
Nigg,		7 50	10 19		12 1r			4 52
Parkhill,		7 59	10 26		12 12			5 0
Delny,		8 6	10 32		12 23			5 6
Invergordon,		8 13	10 45		12 45			5 15
Alness,		8 27	10 54		1 2			5 25
Novar,		8 37	11 4		1 18			5 35
Fowlis,		8 44	11 10		1 29			5 45
Dingwall,		8 57	11 22		1 50			5 57
Conon,		9 4	11 29		2 5			6 3
Muir of Ord,		9 13	11 38		2 25			6 12
Beauly,		9 22	11 47		2 50			6 22
Clunes,		9 28	11 54		3 5			6 32
Lentran,		9 32	11 59		3 26			6 39
Bunchrew,		9 38	12 5					6 45
Arrive at Inverness,		9 50	12 15		P.M. 3 45			7 0

The Class of Trains refer to the Highland Railway Company's Line only.

Second Class Passengers booked from all the principal Stations to Perth and London and *vice versa* by the Trains marked*

Passengers booked to Perth at Parliamentary Fares from Stations north of Inverness by the train leaving Inverness at 12.40 P.M.

CHEAP FARES ON SATURDAYS.

Return Tickets, at a Single Fare, are issued by all the Trains on Saturday, available to return same day, by any Train, or on the Monday following.

THIRD CLASS TO LONDON DAILY a 42s 6d.

Horses and Carriages carried by all the Trains—Limited Mail excepted.
For Passengers Fares, Conditions under which Tickets are issued Coaches in connection, Goods Trains, &c., see the Company's Time Tables

Messrs WORDIE & Co., Agents for the Companies, receive and deliver Goods and Parcels in Bonar Bridge, Clashmore, Dornoch, Golspie, Tain, Invergordon, Dingwall, Avoch, Muir of Ord, Beauly, Inverness, Nairn, Forres, Grantown, Kingussie, Pitlochry, Dunkeld, and Perth, and also Burghead Elgin Fochabe and Keith;
Or
AND DOUGALL, *General Manager*
nverness, 22nd Feb. 1867

a branch to Boat of Garten, and in the eighteen-eighties built a coastal line to serve Portsoy, Cullen, and Buckie which came into Elgin from the seaward side, with its own station in Elgin at its junction with the line from Craigellachie. Here, too, at Elgin North Wordie & Co. established a depot. In 1876 the Great North had taken over the Deeside Line to Ballater which served Balmoral, and independent railways to Peterhead and Fraserburgh were absorbed into what became an efficient system. William Wordie secured the Great North cartage contract in 1869. This led to the increasing importance of his established Aberdeen office, which henceforth had overall responsibility for a growing number of outstations such as Inverurie, Huntly, Fraserburgh, Turriff, Lossiemouth, Portsoy, Cullen and Maud Junction.

Working for the Highland and the Great North of Scotland brought William Wordie a new traffic, whisky. He is believed to have had an early association with Dewar's of Perth, and in the eighteen-eighties Wordie's may have carried their first shipments to England from the Inveralmond distillery to the Dundee, Perth & London Shipping Company's wharf at Perth. It is the tradition that they did.

Beer had long been a regular traffic from the Alloa and Edinburgh breweries, the latter taken to the Caledonian's first terminus in Lothian Road. In 1870 this became goods only when Princes Street passenger station was opened; it was a makeshift affair at first but was fully rebuilt in 1892/93. Otherwise Wordie & Co. carried everything carried by the railway, which then meant everything.

By the eighteen-seventies Wordie's receipts from the Caledonian were considerable: for May, 1870, £223 for work at Aberdeen, £339 for work at Dundee and £208 at Montrose, although Kirriemuir turned in only £19 and Coupar Angus and Blairgowrie combined no more than £18. At about the same time the monthly receipts from the Inverness & Perth, by now called the Highland, were about £50.

William Wordie had two sons and five daughters. John, born in 1839, joined his father in the business round about 1858 after a short spell in the Edinburgh & Glasgow Bank, first in Stirling and then in Glasgow, while Peter, born in 1840, was with a Glasgow grain merchant before he became a partner in the City of Glasgow Brewery. On 9th October, 1874, William Wordie died following a heart attack at his home, Garngabber near Lenzie; he was sixty-five. His obituary in the *Stirling Observer* for 15th October, 1874, said that from 1860 after an uphill struggle his business was flourishing, with by 1874 seven-hundred-odd horses worth some £25,000; the stables had grown in size and number since 1860, to match the work.

By 1877, for example, Wordie & Co. were receiving between £500 and £600 from the Caledonian for a month's work at Dundee. As a contrast, minute receipts were still coming from the North British: for work at Stirling in 1874, seventeen shillings and fourpence and seventeen shillings and sixpence, say 87p in modern money; odd jobs to oblige, possibly to help out Cowan & Co.

In their obituary the *Glasgow Star* said: "Mr Wordie had always a kindly word, and his little, quick, energetic figure will be missed from the platforms of our northern railways."

A chalk drawing of James Glass holding a silver snuff box inscribed "Presented to Mr James Glass by the workmen of Mr William Wordie as a token of esteem. January 1st, 1846". This was early in William Wordie's railway carrying career, and it is possible Mr Glass was the Glasgow manager when the business was still being run from Stirling.
P. J. Wordie

Over the Border and 4
Across the Irish Sea

WITH depots established the length of Scotland and a business allied to what was proving to be the most powerful of the Scottish railways, the Caledonian, and to two others which became models of efficiency, it was still necessary for the company to seek new outlets. An organization which stands still withers, a state far removed from William Wordie's aim. The energy which sent horses and carts to Thurso was not allowed to die; his sons had the ability to maintain his momentum. Peter Wordie left his brewery and came into the family business in 1876 as a partner.

The link with Pickford's was kept as the English outlet, bringing much business, but the only means of expansion in Scotland was to gain contracts with shipping companies, for by the eighteen-seventies railway cartage contracts were all taken up, Wordie & Co. having a major share. By this time Cowan & Co., likewise now with their head office in Glasgow, were the established carting agents for the North British and Glasgow & South Western, while J. & P. Cameron also did North British work. On the eastern side of the country North British cartage was handled by the Dundee firm of Mutter Howey. Smaller firms had contracts with the railway companies in each town and the railways themselves had their own cartage departments.

Scottish geography, however, ensured that many centres offering business could not be reached by rail. By the later nineteenth century the islands and the sea lochs had adequate steamer services; often these services were more than adequate, this being certainly so with the passenger ships. Many more steamer routes radiated from the Clyde than from any other firth, and it was to serve the ships running to and from Glasgow that the two Wordie brothers turned their energies. Their father had shown some interest in shipping in the eighteen-sixties when he took shares in the steamer *Alice* of the Glasgow, Leith & St Petersburg Steam Ship Company.

In 1888 Wordie & Co. contracted to do cartage for the Campbeltown steamers which sailed from the Broomielaw in Glasgow with passengers, mail and cargo to the west coast of Arran and Kintyre. They ran a daily service to Campbeltown, calling at Lochranza and Pirnmill on Arran and Carradale and Saddell on Kintyre, while their calls at Gourock and Greenock offered railway connections with Glasgow. Wordie & Co. limited their work to the

The Campbeltown steamer Davaar, *built of steel at Glasgow in 1885. Wordie & Co. contracted in 1884 to do the cartage for the Campbeltown & Glasgow Steam Packet Joint Stock Co. Ltd at their Broomielaw berth, and followed this by contracts with other shipping lines.*

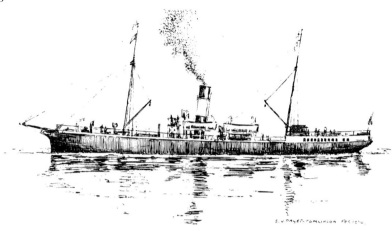

Broomielaw berth, the contract lasting until nationalization, although by 1948 the shipping company had undergone several changes of control: founded in 1826, it was best known as the Campbeltown & Glasgow Steam Packet Joint Stock Company Ltd.

More adventurous was the 1888 contract with Messrs G. & J. Burns of Glasgow. James and George Burns had started a Glasgow–Belfast steamer service in 1826 and a Glasgow–Liverpool steamer three years later. By the late eighteen-sixties, there were sailings to Londonderry and from 1878 to Larne, while in 1882 G. & J. Burns acquired the Ardrossan Shipping Company, giving them a second route to Belfast. In 1908 Burns entered the Dublin trade by purchase of the Dublin & Glasgow Sailing and Steam Packet Company. Wordie & Co.'s first contract was for the Londonderry and Larne steamers; they followed this up in 1897 with one for the Glasgow–Belfast steamers, which it seems from the Post Office Directories was shared with Cowan & Co. In 1909 Wordie & Co. added work for Burns' Dublin steamers in Glasgow. This activity introduced Wordie's to the Irish trade, and soon they were established in Ireland itself; indeed cartage in Ireland was by 1914 a major part of their business.

Meanwhile more shipping contracts were gained. Wordie & Co.'s work in Aberdeen brought them in touch with the North of Scotland, Orkney & Shetland Steam Navigation Company, an old-established concern which had served the Orkneys and Shetlands with their steamers since 1836, being given a mail contract two years later. They ran from Leith via Aberdeen and called also at Wick and Thurso, Wordie & Co. providing cartage at all four places. The North Company contracts, gained in 1889, stayed with Wordie & Co. until nationalization.

Two more shipping companies relied on Wordie & Co. In 1892 the company gained a cartage contract with the Great

Northern Railway of Ireland in Belfast. They followed this up in 1897 by agreeing to work in Belfast for the Belfast & Mersey Steamship Company, which had been founded in 1883; this company later merged with the Liverpool owners J. J. Mack and much later, in 1930, with the Belfast & Manchester Steamship Company to form the Belfast, Mersey and Manchester Steamship Company. These were the Liverpool steamers, as Wordie's in Belfast called them; not to be confused with the Belfast Steamship Company, which ran the Belfast–Liverpool passenger ships as well as cargo services and handled their own cartage.

Secondly and also in 1897 Wordie & Co. began to work for the Glasgow firm J. & P. Hutchison, founded in the mid eighteen-fifties to run between Scotland, Ireland and France. The links with France became particularly strong, to the extent of the company's carrying medical supplies free during the Franco-Prussian War; they were rewarded by the tricolour houseflag defaced by the Scottish thistle. In 1934 J. & P. Hutchison merged with James Moss of Liverpool to become the Moss-Hutchison Line.

Cartage for the Great Northern Railway of Ireland started in Belfast on 1st August, 1892, and was expanded over most of their system. This was an enterprising and progressive railway created in 1876 out of a group of smaller companies which had between them built the railway between Belfast and Dublin, opened in 1855, and another group which by 1859 had reached Londonderry via Enniskillen and constructed a considerable network of lines to

Newry station with a Belfast train headed by one of the T2 class of 4-4-2 tanks waiting to leave. Having become established in Belfast as carriers for the Great Northern, Wordie & Co. opened depots elsewhere on the system; there was one at Newry by the turn of the century.

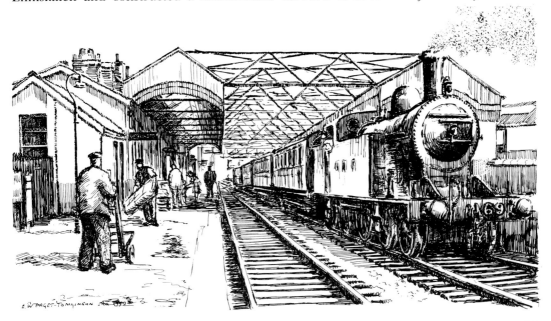

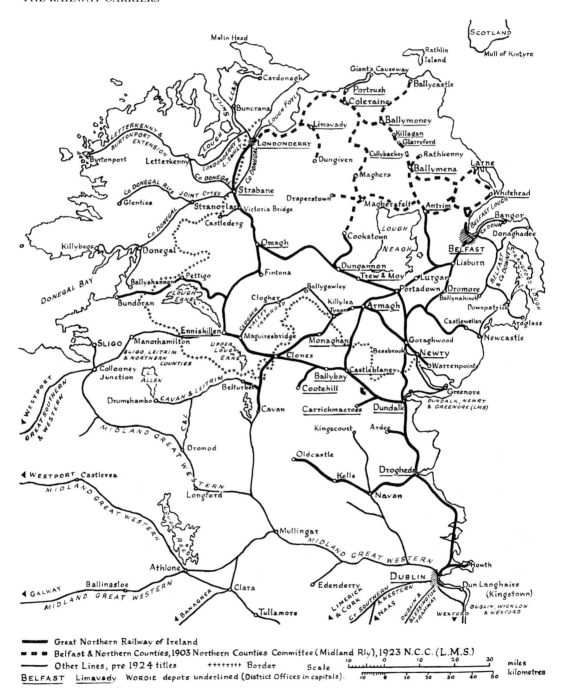

SCOTLAND
Mull of Kintyre

Malin Head
Rathlin Island
Giant's Causeway
Cardonagh
Portrush
Ballycastle
Coleraine
Buncrana
Limavady
Ballymoney
LETTERKENNY & BURTONPORT EXTENSION
Killagan
Glarryford
LOUGH FOYLE
LONDONDERRY
Dungiven
Cullybackey
Rathkenny
Burtonport
Letterkenny
Maghera
Ballymena
Larne
Whitehead
Co DONEGAL RLYS JOINT CTTEE
Strabane
Draperstown
Magherafelt
Antrim
BELFAST LOUGH
Bangor
Glenties
Stranorlar
Victoria Bridge
Donaghadee
Castlederg
Cookstown
LOUGH NEAGH
BELFAST
Killybegs
Donegal
Omagh
Lisburn
Dromore
DONEGAL BAY
Fintona
Dungannon
Trew & Moy
Lurgan
Ballynahinch
Downpatrick
Ballyshannon
Pettigo
Ballygawley
Portadown
Bundoran
LOUGH ERNE
Clogher
Killylea
Tynan
Armagh
Castlewellan
Newcastle
Ardglass
SLIGO
Manorhamilton
Enniskillen
CLOGHER VALLEY TRAMROAD
Maguiresbridge
Monaghan
Goraghwood
Collooney Junction
UPPER LOUGH ERNE
Clones
Bessbrook
Newry
Warrenpoint
SLIGO, LEITRIM & NORTHERN COUNTIES
LL. ALLEN
Castleblaney
Greenore
Drumshambo
CAVAN & LEITRIM
Belturbet
Ballybay
Cootehill
DUNDALK, NEWRY & GREENORE (LMS)
WESTPORT GREAT SOUTHERN & WESTERN
Cavan
Carrickmacross
Dundalk
Kingscourt
Ardee
Dromod
Oldcastle
MIDLAND GREAT WESTERN
WESTPORT Castlerea
Kells
Drogheda
MIDLAND GREAT WESTERN
Longford
Navan
Mullingar
MIDLAND GREAT WESTERN
Athlone
Howth
GALWAY
Ballinasloe
MIDLAND GREAT WESTERN
Clara
Edenderry
DUBLIN
Dun Laoghaire (Kingstown)
BANAGHER
Tullamore
LIMERICK & CORK
GT SOUTHERN & WESTERN
NAAS
DUBLIN & BLESSINGTON TRAMWAY
WEXFORD
DUBLIN, WICKLOW & WEXFORD

────── Great Northern Railway of Ireland
- - - - Belfast & Northern Counties, 1903 Northern Counties Committee (Midland Rly), 1923 N.C.C. (L.M.S.)
────── Other Lines, pre 1924 titles   ++++++++ Border   Scale
BELFAST Limavady WORDIE depots underlined (District Offices in capitals).

miles
kilometres

34

serve most of the towns of the North, then and for many years integral with the rest of Ireland. In Belfast the Great Northern had three goods stations: Grosvenor Street was the main one and there were two smaller, Maysfield and Queensbridge. To provide the cartage for an ever-busier traffic, Wordie & Co. built stables at Lagan Bank Road, and then in Divis Street, these latter becoming the principal ones. Apart from collection and delivery round the city there was much interchange traffic between the Great Northern goods stations and those of other companies, the Belfast & Northern Counties at York Road and the Belfast & County Down at Queen's Quay, as well as parcels traffic from the Great Northern passenger station at Great Victoria Street.

The Belfast & Northern Counties was another amalgamation of lines from Belfast to Ballymena, Ballymoney, Coleraine, Portrush and Londonderry, all opened by 1855, the Carrickfergus & Larne following in 1862. It was in competition with the Great Northern for Londonderry traffic and met the latter at two other places, Antrim and Cookstown. In 1903 the Northern Counties was bought by the English Midland Railway, who in 1904 opened their new port for the Irish trade at Heysham and built four ships to run between Heysham and Belfast and Heysham and Douglas. Acquisition of a railway in Ulster assured the Midland of substantial traffic for their new ships and port.

Finally there was the small County Down Railway serving Co. Down and the coast, opened to Hollywood in 1848, Bangor in 1865 and Downpatrick and Newcastle in 1869; the Bangor and Newcastle lines were built by independent companies eventually bought by the County Down. Cartage was done for this railway by the Scottish rivals Cowan & Co., who had moved across to Ireland in 1877 and gained a contract with the County Down in 1895, having in 1889 won the Belfast cartage work for the Belfast–Fleetwood steamers operated jointly by the London & North Western and Lancashire & Yorkshire railways in England.

Work for the Great Northern in Belfast was followed, as in Scotland, by the setting up of depots elsewhere on the system, at Londonderry and Enniskillen, at Strabane, Omagh, Dungannon, Armagh, Newry, Carrickmacross and later, in 1900 and 1902, at Dundalk and Drogheda. By 1902 they were in Dublin itself, working from Amiens Street station, with stables in Ossory Road by the Royal Canal on the northern side of the city and an office in Westmoreland Street in the centre, moving to Beresford Place near Amiens Street after 1918. Wordie & Co. also acted for the Lancashire & Yorkshire Railway in Dublin; this link was an offshoot, it must be imagined, from their long-standing Pickford's connection which provided the link with the English railway companies.

Railways in the northern half of Ireland served by Wordie & Co., Wordie & Co. (Ulster) Ltd, and Wordie & Co. (Dublin). There were only two out-stations to Dublin, Drogheda and Dundalk, the remainder coming under Belfast and Londonderry. The latter for a while served as a district office.

35

A London & North Western express on the West Coast route to Scotland picking up water from troughs between the lines. Because F. W. Webb's engines were never powerful enough for the work they had to do, double-heading was everyday practice on the LNWR, for whom Wordie & Co. acted as agents in Scotland.

There were other small Great Northern stations where the cartage was done by locals under contract to Wordie & Co. These were at Dromore in Co. Tyrone and several places in Co. Cavan and Co. Monaghan. The smallest depot seems to have been at Trew and Moy station near Dungannon in Co. Tyrone, where according to a 1931 survey there was work for only one-fifth of a horse.

After 1932 the Dublin business, which included the depots in what was by then the Irish Free State, was formed into a separate company; work at Drogheda was given up in 1934 and at Dundalk in 1935. Wordie & Co. remained in Dublin until 1946/47 (they had bought their last horses in 1941), when the business was sold to a concern called Transport and Storage Ltd.

By the time work began in Belfast for the Great Northern, and possibly well before, Wordie & Co. had secured another railway contract in Scotland which served the Irish trade. This was with the Portpatrick & Wigtownshire line, which ran from Castle Douglas to Portpatrick and Stranraer, fully open in 1862. From these ports the crossing to Ireland was the shortest possible in mileage, and steamers had been on the route since 1825. Portpatrick, however, remained a difficult harbour to enter in spite of improvements and the service remained unsatisfactory until in 1872 sheltered Stranraer was in permanent use. By then five railway companies supported the steamers, the London & North Western, Midland, Caledonian, Glasgow & South Western, and the Belfast & Northern Counties (which joined the Midland in 1903), operating as the Larne & Stranraer Steamship Joint Committee. Of these railways, two became responsible for the Portpatrick & Wigtownshire; from 1885 it became a joint line under the operating control of the Glasgow & South Western and the Caledonian, who took turns to work it for three-year periods. Financial interest in the line was also held by the London & North Western and the Midland. For Wordie & Co., who appear to have had a depot in Stranraer as early as 1866, the Portpatrick & Wigtownshire brought work with the Larne steamers.

Because the Caledonian and the London & North Western formed the West Coast route between England and Scotland, Wordie & Co. as Caledonian agents and through their Pickford's connection also acted for the London & North Western in Scotland as well as for other English railways such as the Lancashire & Yorkshire. From 1896 they themselves entered the cartage business in England when they opened a depot in Newcastle-upon-Tyne as Caledonian agents, gaining a contract in 1904 with the powerful North Eastern Railway. This was enemy territory, for the North-Eastern was the core of the East Coast route between England and Scotland, their northern partner being the North British. At the same time Wordie's kept on their Caledonian work in Newcastle and acquired many customers of their own.

This was as well, because at the 1923 railway grouping the new London & North Eastern cancelled the North Eastern contract, although Wordie & Co. were able to keep the Caledonian work when that railway was absorbed into the London, Midland & Scottish. Eventually in 1937, by which time Wordie's were under

The paddle steamer Princess Victoria of 1890, the first vessel built by Denny of Dumbarton for the Stranraer–Larne route. Stranraer proved a rewarding centre for Wordie cartage after it had replaced Portpatrick as the Scottish terminal for the Larne steamers, which were designed for both passengers and cattle. Denny's were told to conceal the presence of the cattle from passengers; this demanded a special ventilation system, although it has to be admitted that only a canvas screen separated the steerage passengers from the beasts.

E.W. PAGET-TOMLINSON JAN 1990.

37

LMS control, Newcastle's biggest road carrier Currie & Co., who worked for the LNER, took over Wordie's Newcastle operations, with the concurrence of the LMS, and established a subsidiary which kept the Wordie name, Wordie & Co. (Newcastle) Ltd.

In spite of expansion—by 1905 the company must have owned nearly three thousand horses—the nineteen-hundreds were a difficult decade for the cartage industry, with much labour unrest. Labour was by now becoming organized, with stronger union representation, and the employers were faced with constant and justified wage demands. In her book *The Scottish Carter* (Allen & Unwin, 1967), Angela Tuckett has recorded the fights of the Scottish Horse and Motormen's Association to gain fair rewards for their members. The union was founded in 1898 at a time of trade depression and unemployment. There had been a big carters' strike in Glasgow in 1889, but few demands were met, none at all for the benefit of the railway carters. However, Wordie & Co. and Cowan & Co. along with other employers did grant a wage increase of a shilling (5p) a week in 1899; wages at this time were between nineteen and twenty-five shillings a week, that is between 95p and £1.25, for a week of up to seventy-five hours.

Starting time then was four or five in the morning and finishing was at eight or nine at night; much of this time was spent standing around at stations waiting turns to load or deliver. Sunday work to feed, water and muck out was also expected, and, most serious of all, men were responsible for breakage and loss of goods, which they had to make up out of their own pockets. This included theft from lorries. There was an advantage here for the workers, oddly enough: if the men owed money they had to be kept on.

There was a strike at Falkirk in 1902 by Wordie and Cowan

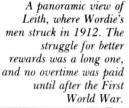

A panoramic view of Leith, where Wordie's men struck in 1912. The struggle for better rewards was a long one, and no overtime was paid until after the First World War.

A Caledonian Railway express hauled by a 4-4-0 engine of the "Dunalastair" class. It was as agents for the Caledonian that Wordie & Co. opened a depot at Newcastle-upon-Tyne in 1896.

men and another by railway carters in Glasgow in 1911; Leith men struck in 1912. In 1907 there had been a strike in Belfast, and there were plenty more to follow. Gradually the men achieved a better reward, although the hours remained long, with no overtime paid until after 1918. As soon as wage increases were met the employers pressed the railway companies for an increase in rates.

There was a fear that if cartage rates became too high customers would do their own cartage. They had to be wooed off this by attractive rebates from the cartage companies. Surviving correspondence between Wordie & Co. in Belfast and the Great Northern Railway reflects the constant battle for increased rates, with complaints about congestion and waiting at the goods stations. There was a shortage of railway wagons and of porters on the Great Northern in those pre-1914 years; traffic was on the increase and carters were finding they had to do much of the portering. Someone calculated that it would take a Belfast carter an average of one hour twenty-six minutes to discharge his load at a station, a load which would not be more than a couple of tons, usually much less, but made up of small items, each of which had to be shifted singly.

Nevertheless, Wordie & Co. were expanding. In 1903 they took over the Glasgow carriers R. Grierson & Co. and at the same time set up a property company to look after their stables and depots and the houses of their staff, which were often adjacent to their yards. This expanded into a property development company involved with shops and streets on an increasing scale; a typical project was Bannermill in Aberdeen. By this time their head office

John Wordie (1839–1910), who joined his father in the business about 1858, was highly regarded as a collector of art.
P. J. Wordie

was in West Nile Street in Glasgow, moving in the nineteen-thirties to Buchanan Street and finally to West George Street.

R. Grierson & Co. were a useful acquisition. Their office was in Wellington Street in Glasgow and they had stables in Stirling Street, Port Dundas Road and Bishop Street in Glasgow as well as in Paisley, because they had a contract with the Glasgow & Paisley Joint Railway, the main route between Glasgow and Paisley, whose control was shared between those arch enemies the Caledonian and the Glasgow & South Western. The same two companies also shared the neighbouring Glasgow, Barrhead & Kilmarnock, whose cartage was done by Cowan & Co. But the main attraction of Grierson's to the Wordies was their shipping work, cartage in Glasgow for G. & J. Burns' Liverpool steamers, for Langlands' Glasgow–Manchester steamers, for the Carron Company, who ran passenger and cargo ships to Hull, King's Lynn and London. Normally the Carron ships ran from Leith, but some sailings were from Glasgow.

Grierson's had ninety-two horses on their acquisition and a variety of vehicles, including four carts for carrying chemical carboys and a furniture van. Their sole partner was George Robb, the same George Robb surely who had become the Caledonian's first carting superintendent in 1870. Now he and John and Peter Wordie assumed three equal shares in the Grierson concern, but when he died in 1909 the company became wholly Wordie. An early acquisition under the new partnership was a Yorkshire steam wagon bought in 1905 for £403; it was sold after only five years. Grierson's were kept as an independent business but made steady losses, sometimes heavy ones, although they did become profitable by the nineteen-thirties. They remained a subsidiary until 1948, when the cartage activities were given up; the company remained in being a further year as an investment business.

On 26th December, 1910, John Wordie died and the partnership was re-formed with his elder son William and his nephew Archibald Watson (the latter had been with the company since 1897) joining his brother Peter, their uncle, although Peter no longer took an active part in the business. John Wordie was highly regarded as a connoisseur and collector of oil and watercolour paintings and particularly of etchings. His advice was sought on the mounting of exhibitions; in 1911 he was due to go to Rome to assist in the assembly of an art exhibition of international standing, but this was a task he could not undertake. His other interest was in Scottish proverbs, about which he built up a considerable library. His obituary in the *Glasgow Herald* speaks of his association with the Glasgow Fine Arts Club; like his father he was a Son of the Rock, an 1871 amalgamation of two charitable and social societies of men of Stirlingshire resident in Glasgow, established in 1809 and 1865 respectively, to aid the poor of Stirlingshire, to award bursaries and prizes at the Stirling High School and more recently the University and to enjoy an annual dinner. He had been educated in Stirling and Glasgow, and recalled in an address as an Old Boy of Stirling High School in 1898 how in the fifties it was common for the boys to volunteer for work at the local slaughterhouse.

A more homely detail has come down about him from a recent correspondent, Mrs Sheena Crook, of Clarkston, Glasgow. She writes:

> My mother, when she was a young girl (around 1900), was an assistant in the then-well-known firm of Mann, Byars & Co., Virginia Street, and one of their customers was Mrs Wordie (herself a Mann) . . .
>
> When we were children and received a parcel my mother would not let us cut the string but made us untie the knots and keep the string to be used again, telling us the story of how Mrs Wordie came into her department one day to exchange some garment. My mother being young and anxious not to keep a customer waiting reached for the scissors to cut the string. Mrs Wordie took the parcel from her saying, "Girl, never waste string, that's how my husband made his money, by being thrifty." It became a byword in our home as we watched mother carefully untying knots; we smiled and said, "Remember Mrs Wordie". I still use the expression.

John Wordie's investment portfolio has survived in the company ledgers. Apart from the highly regarded railway shares, "blue chips" in those days, John Wordie held stock in shipping companies such as the Aberdeen, Newcastle & Hull Steam Company and in the ill-fated La Platense Flotilla, an attempt by Denny's to do for the River Plate what they had achieved on the Irrawaddy. He was keen on hotel investment at Portree, Gairloch in Ross-shire and Bridge of Allan, and put money in concerns associated with his business such as the Glasgow Horse Slaughtering Company, shades of his schooldays activities.

His funeral was, as one would expect, attended by the railway hierarchy of Scotland. The service at his parish church in Glasgow, Hyndland, was followed by interment at Stirling, where all the Wordies are buried; a special train left Buchanan Street to carry the coffin to Stirling. On the way up to the cemetery from Stirling station the blinds of all the shops were lowered and the doors closed.

With his eldest son in the business there was no problem of family continuity of management, although his brother Peter had no children. His nephew Archie Watson was the elder son of another carrier, Archibald Watson, who had married his sister Anne. John Wordie's younger son James was at this time an undergraduate at Cambridge, where he read geology. In 1914 he

Archie Watson, a nephew of John Wordie and the son of another carrier, joined the business in 1897. P. J. Wordie

41

Peter Wordie (1840–1913), from a miniature painted in the year he died. P. J. Wordie

joined Sir Ernest Shackleton's expedition to cross the Antarctic Continent as senior scientist, sailing south in the *Endurance* just after the outbreak of war.

By this time Peter Wordie too had gone. A more flamboyant character than his brother, Peter owned a steam yacht which he used for company meetings, anchored in Dublin Bay or Belfast Lough. He died on 26th June, 1913, and left the bulk of his large fortune to charity. His will was contested by the family and the case reached the House of Lords, who in 1916 upheld the decision of the Court of Session that the will was valid. Although John also left a sizable fortune the abstraction of so much capital provoked a financial crisis within the partnership. Money was raised from members of the family, for example James Wordie, and the business carried on into the 1914–18 War with Archie Watson, the senior partner, in charge. William Wordie joined the army; he was commissioned into the Army Service Corps and posted to Egypt, where his transport knowledge ensured him a place on the Arab Bureau in Cairo, the office which organized T. E. Lawrence's supply line through Jeddah.

At home the railways were from the outbreak of war in August, 1914, put under Government control as a single system under a Railway Executive Committee, and their cartage agents with them. All were hard pressed, but none more so than the Highland, on which the Grand Fleet at Scapa depended. Highland locomotives and rolling stock had to be augmented from other railways, the coal traffic being the biggest problem. Delays were considerable and local distribution suffered, but the Wordie organization remained intact, although many men were called up; some did not return.

Peace in 1918 left an exhausted railway system which could not

William Wordie (1884–1952) in the uniform of the Army Service Corps, in which he served during the First World War. P. J. Wordie

go back to the rivalries of the pre-1914 years, with many small and unprofitable concerns and needless competition. Following the Railways Act of 1921, which usefully clarified the railways' road haulage powers, the railways of mainland Britain were for the most part grouped into four radiating from London, ideas for a separate Scottish railway being abandoned. Instead Scotland was divided between two companies: the new London, Midland & Scottish took over the Caledonian, the Glasgow & South Western and the Highland, also the Portpatrick & Wigtownshire and the joint lines from Glasgow to Paisley and Kilmarnock, while the new London & North Eastern captured the North British and the Great North of Scotland. The groups, which were independent companies without state backing, came alive on 1st January, 1923.

For Wordie & Co. there was a division of loyalty. Their agreements with the Caledonian and the Highland put them in the London, Midland & Scottish camp, likewise with the Portpatrick & Wigtownshire. Their contract with the Great North of Scotland brought them under the wing of the rival London & North Eastern, who were mainly served by the ex-North British carriers Cowan & Co., Mutter Howey & Co. and, until 1926, J. & P. Cameron. This presented a strange situation, although the LNER worked their Great North of Scotland section as a near-independent railway, as geographically it was; the LNER only had running powers into Aberdeen from the south, from Kinnaber Junction near Montrose.

In Ireland the Midland-owned Belfast & Northern Counties came within the LMS group as the London, Midland & Scottish Railway, Northern Counties Committee; the Midland was a principal constituent of the LMS. This title of Northern Counties Committee had been bestowed on the Belfast & Northern Counties when it was bought in 1903 and remained throughout LMS ownership; it was rarely used, since "Midland" and then "LMS" were the normal conversational titles. The establishment of the Irish Free State in 1921 and the creation of the Province of Northern Ireland divided the Great Northern of Ireland between two countries; the other major railways in the Free State combined in 1924–25 to form Great Southern Railways. Wordie & Co., however, had agreements at this stage only with the Great Northern, but work for the LMS in Ulster was soon to follow, as Chapter nine will explain.

The early nineteen-twenties are a good time to break off strict historical continuity and to examine the nature of the business. This is recalled by people who have written and talked about their work with memories which inevitably go no further back than the nineteen-twenties. The following four chapters therefore are theirs, historical continuity returning with Chapter nine.

Management and 5
Operation

TO PROVIDE an efficient cartage service for a large railway company such as the Caledonian, not only were horses and carts needed in quantity but local roads had to stand up to the wear of multitudes of iron-shod hooves and iron-tyred wheels. Cobbles and from the mid-eighteenth century granite setts were laid, the gaps between the setts—cassies or causeys in Scotland (an abbreviation of causeway)—giving the horses purchase, traction sometimes being aided by three-foot wooden baulks laid crosswise on steep hills, for example in Dundee, at the right interval for the horses' feet, while iron plates were often laid to provide a smoother passage for the wheels.

Aberdeen was the home of the cassie-making industry, as John McLaren, the historian of Aberdeen granite, explains. Six hundred men were employed on this by the seventeen-nineties, the peak of the industry being reached in the eighteen-sixties; the industry died in the nineteen-twenties. The noise of iron tyres on cassies, well remembered by many Wordie & Co. families, was deafening. Some cities like London laid hardwood blocks to reduce the noise, but on quaysides, railway goods yard forecourts and in the lanes leading to forge and factory the cobbles and setts or cassies reigned supreme.

For urban and local cartage work the horse was at an advantage, for it was nimble, with great manoeuvrability, and able to start and stop at an instant. Speed was not a prime factor, nor was weight carrying, but the need to turn and back was paramount. Journeys were short, well within the capacity of a healthy horse, which could work for up to twelve hours a day. With the hindsight of decades of mechanical road transport, the shortcomings of horses can be seen: their need to eat and sleep, their ailments, their short range, low power and low speed. But in the nineteenth century there were no alternatives and therefore no disadvantages.

Agricultural improvement in the eighteenth century, better roads in the early nineteenth and later the cartage demands of the railways fostered the breeding of draught horses. In Scotland the native strain was the Lanarkshire Clydesdale, sustained by stallions from Flanders and England, the latter being Shires from the Midlands. The Clydesdale had the merit of brisk action, with a long quick step well suited to railway delivery work, and smart acceleration after the frequent stops. Slower Shire blood gave

Opposite page:
Looking down Schoolhill, Aberdeen, with the entrance to Wordie's stables next to Lockhart's shop on the left; the words "Wordie & Co." appear above the entrance.
Aberdeen University Library, George Washington Wilson Collection Ref D 2006

strength. It is admitted today that Shires and Clydesdales are mixed up, in spite of the founding of the Clydesdale Society in 1877. An average Clydesdale stands 16.2 hands; the Shire is bigger, 16.2 to 17.2 hands, with a weight of up to 22 hundredweight. Clydesdales are dark brown, black or bay, black ones being preferred; the white markings on the legs and face are signs of purity. Wordie & Co. had many Clydesdales, Shires too, Irish Draught horses, cross Percherons and some Belgian animals. For lighter work they had Irish Gyp horses, crosses between Irish Draught horses and Connemaras, lighter horses with less hairy feet, and for the vans they had the vanners or "trotting" horses of 15.2 hands or so. Talking of size, one 19-hand horse is remembered in Belfast.

Draught horses have a life of nine to twelve years in harness, starting at the age of three to five and continuing to twelve or fifteen. Replenishment was a constant need, particularly for a large cartage business such as Wordie & Co. Some of their horse records have survived, including a register or "horse book" which goes back to 1858 and onwards to 1954, see appendix four. The bulk of the book is a list of purchases, year by year up to 1932 but from and including that year a daily record, though only of the horses bought by the non-LMS side of the business. This gives the date of purchase, the serial number of the purchase on that day, the seller, a description of the animal including age, the cost, the depot to

A stable scene, showing the stalls, the moss peat litter, and the gears hanging ready for the day's work. To the right a foot examination is in progress.

E.W. PAGET-TOMLINSON DEC '89

Alex Reiach with Jock at Maud, on the Great North of Scotland line between Aberdeen and Fraserburgh.
Alex Reiach

which the horse was assigned, distinguishing marks, the horse's official stock number branded on a fore hoof, and a note of the page in the record book in which the horse's career was recorded. There is also a remarks column which generally says simply "paid" but occasionally notes a horse which had to be returned to the seller for one reason or another.

One can do no better than quote an actual example. On 31st January, 1934, W. C. Allan of Inverurie sold a brown six-year-old gelding for £72 to Wordie & Co. He was stabled at their Inverurie depot and was distinguished by a broad stripe on the face and white legs. His hoof number was 44. Later he moved to Huntly, where on 7th February, 1943, his carcase was sold for £9 (his stock value reckoned as £6) after he had died from lymphangitis and heart disease. The dead horse records are separate at the back of the book and are interesting for their notes on the causes of death. Lymphangitis is an inflammation affecting the legs causing acute lameness, usually in one hindleg, rarely in a foreleg. It was not fatal; indeed it was common in working horses after an idle weekend, hence the name generally used among horsemen, Monday morning disease.

Mr R. M. McCaughey was a student veterinary surgeon at

Wordie horse lorries loading cans of fish fry from the fish farm at Howietoun near Stirling for despatch from Stirling station in the eighteen-nineties. The farm was founded in 1874 and flourishes today under the University of Stirling. Wordie involvement was deeper than transport, because the farm bought old horses for fish feed. All this is described by Tom Lannon in The Story of Howietoun, *published by the University in 1989.* University of Stirling.

Ballymena in Northern Ireland in the nineteen-forties. Much of his time was spent at the Wordie stables there and he remembers seeing both lymphangitis and laminitis, which is inflammation of the foot, treated by large doses of raw linseed oil and a starvation diet, followed after the resultant purgation by graduated exercise. Laminitis could also be treated by steeping the leg in hot and cold water alternately, steeping tubs being standard stable equipment. Most common causes of death according to the records were twisted bowels, ruptures of the stomach and intestines, heart failure, broken limbs, and "worn out". Generally the horses are noted as destroyed.

Sometimes horses were returned to the seller, usually because they proved to be poor workers, but very few failed to give satisfaction; only thirteen between December, 1932, and June, 1944, as listed in the horse book. The death rate averaged six or seven a year in the nineteen-thirties, although in 1937 they lost as many as fourteen, all but one in Ireland. One has to remember when looking at these figures that they refer only to the non-LMS side of the business; for the whole company they would be much greater.

On the other hand horses were frequently sold for further service if they were no longer needed, or surplus. An advertisement in the *Aberdeen Journal* of 31st October, 1860, announces a sale at the Wordie stables, then in Gas Lane, Aberdeen, of twenty to thirty horses to take place on 9th November. They came from the Scottish North Eastern Railway, with whom Wordie's had had a

[A facsimile of two handwritten pages from the Wordie's "horse book" ledger, headed "Horses Dead" / "Wordie (North Eastern) Ltd", recording horse deaths with columns for Date, Station, Description, Cost, and Cause of Death.]

A pair of pages from the "horse book" listing deaths at the Wordie's (North Eastern) stables from 1939 to 1945. Below is an example of the horse's official number branded on to one of the fore hooves: No 267 was a five-year-old dark brown Irish horse with a star and snip on the nose, white hind legs and black fore legs, bought on 18th December, 1945, from James Bunting and working in Belfast. The Wordie Property Co. Ltd.

cartage contract since its formation by amalgamation in 1856. A few were advertised as suitable for farm or further draught work; others one assumes were not, and would be bought by the knacker to be rendered down for their fat and tallow. Most probably Wordie & Co. had acquired these railway horses as part of the contract, but preferred to build up their own stable.

The number of horses bought reflects the expansion of William Wordie's cartage business. The earliest date in the surviving horse book is 1858, when forty-four horses were bought at an average price of £28 2s (£28.10). But in 1865, the year the Caledonian took over the Scottish Central and the lines to Dundee and Aberdeen, William Wordie bought 117 horses. In 1869, when he gained the work for the Great North of Scotland Railway, he bought 116 horses. The ledgers reveal the names of some dealers; Peter Scott of Dollar and William Walker of Stirling are often mentioned.

In the eighteen-nineties Wordie & Co. were usually buying upwards of 300 horses a year. By this time they were carting for the Great Northern Railway of Ireland, for G. & J. Burns' steamers, for Hutchison's continental steamers, not forgetting Stranraer and the Portpatrick & Wigtownshire Railway. They had also opened their depot in Newcastle. Similar numbers were bought during the nineteen-hundreds, the maximum being reached in 1919 when they purchased 576 horses. Prices remained steady: £58 was the average in both 1879 and 1930. Here is another specific example: on 13th March, 1876, horse No 519 was bought from Peter Scott

E.W.P-T.

for £54. He would not be called 519 at the stable but Blackie or Patch or Blossom. In the nineteen-twenties and -thirties with the lessening of business and the increase in motor transport, horse purchases dropped away: 166 in 1928, 46 in 1933, by the non-LMS side, remember, 23 in 1936, although Wordie & Co. (Ulster) Ltd bought some at the outbreak of the Second World War, 34 between September, 1939, and April, 1940.

By the nineteen-thirties sales were in the hands of a limited band of dealers. One was William C. Allan of Inverurie, who was succeeded from 1944 by Andrew D. Allan, most likely his son. James H. Wilson of Aberdeen remembers William Allan, who generally sold horses twice yearly, sometimes as many as eight or sixteen at a time, but in 1934 two in January and two in April only. Prices were between £50 and £70 for five and six year olds, more expensive than those charged by the Irish dealers, among whom the busiest was William McMullen, of Portaferry at the mouth of Strangford Lough in Co. Down. In 1934 he sold thirty-six horses for work in Belfast and Dublin; most were in the £50 region, a few as much as £60, including a fine black Clydesdale. Colours varied; reading down a column at random there are brown, dark bay, dappled grey, brown roan, chestnut, light dapple grey, all faithfully recorded in the horse book. A horse described as a flea-bitten grey caused consternation in the Glasgow office, where it was thought the horse actually had fleas; all that was meant was a grey horse flecked with spots of brown.

Other dealers noted were John Crawford of Beith in Ayrshire, Arthur Forster of Carlisle, and two from Belfast, James Bunting and Miles Broadbent. Carlisle was a great horse-trading centre with several Clydesdale breeders in the area. Among them were the Kilpatricks of Wigton in Cumberland, whose horses were sold by

Horses from Canada landed at Merklands Dock, Glasgow, in 1936. They came from the Montreal stockyards and were led three abreast to Westerhill Farm, Bishopbriggs, near Glasgow, where George Knox broke them in. They were sold to Glasgow cartage firms, including Wordie's. Douglas Knox

George Knox, who sold horses to Wordie's from his farm at Westerhill, Bishopbriggs, outside Glasgow, poses with one of his horses.
Douglas Knox

Messrs. Harrison & Hetherington of Carlisle, a firm dating from 1877 who may well have had Wordie & Co. among their customers. Nearer home was George Knox of Westerhill Farm, Bishopbriggs, near Glasgow, who bred Clydesdales and imported cross Percherons from Canada. His son, Douglas Knox, recalls three shipments from the Montreal stockyards, the first in 1936 when about thirty horses came over, averaging about sixteen or seventeen hands. They were landed by the Cunard at Merklands Dock in Glasgow and led three abreast to Bishopbriggs, some eight miles away. There George Knox broke them in.

Often horses were transferred from depots belonging to the LMS side, Wordie & Co. Ltd., for example from Aberdeen. Some were older animals; one which went to their Banff stable in October, 1934, was fifteen and cost Banff £4. These transfers indicate that Aberdeen were reducing their horses as they built up their motor fleet.

James Wilson, who recalls the Inverurie horse dealer William Allan, started in February, 1934, as sixth stable boy with Wordie & Co. in Aberdeen. He was then sixteen. After a couple of years he moved on to the motors, first as second man, then as driver until 1958, when he was promoted to cartage supervisor with British Railways at Aberdeen. He retired in 1978, but, like so many who have contributed to this history, his memories of Wordie & Co. are considerable. Horse sales were direct to individual stables, and soon after arrival one of the horse's fore hooves was branded with

Well remembered in Glasgow were Wordie's trace horses at the foot of West Nile Street, waiting to help horses up the hill to the north. This 1930 scene remained familiar until the Second World War. The trace boys sit in a nearby doorway. From *Glasgow Old and New* by Jack House, 1974, with the kind permission of the author.

his or her official number. Most of them were geldings but there was no particular preference between them and mares. Raymond Eddie's mare Darkie, it will be remembered, was a biter and had to be muzzled. Instead of a leather muzzle a horse could have a check chain from the bit to the girth. Kickers were restrained by a kicking strap fitted across the rump. Kicking was generally the result of ill-treatment, severely punished by Wordie's, but only one case has been mentioned.

This is remembered by Eddie McCaffery of Edinburgh, who was a trace boy with Wordie & Co. in 1937. He says a carter had stopped to light the lamps, but the horse, anxious to go home, kept moving on. In anger the carter struck at him with a lamp. A lady who had seen the incident followed the lorry down to Lothian Road goods station, where she reported it to the station manager, who sacked the carter on the spot. Sometimes, says Raymond Eddie, younger men would use the whip on older horses to try to make them work harder. They were reprimanded for this and told they would be given a younger horse when they could look after it.

Most recall how well fed, well groomed and well mannered Wordie & Co. horses were, although there is evidence of some meanness over the diet, with kindly carters supplementing the rations out of their own pockets. Nevertheless, although cartage was a business with little room for sentiment, the horses were loved. Many a carter would stay overnight with his horse if he was sick, like Robert McIntyre, the father of Mrs Kathleen Mills, who will

soon be introduced. Caring made sound economic sense; the animal would work harder, rewarding the care with willingness and obedience. But there was more to it than this. So much time was spent together by the man and his horse, and it was always the same horse, that a bond of affection grew up, trust on both sides, and responsiveness; the man would understand the whims and foibles of the horse and the horse understood the foibles of the man, notably if he was a newly-refreshed carter on brewery work. Some Belfast men, says Joe Galway, who was a carter, took their horses into the pubs, or at least into the door, although they did not drink Guinness.

Wordie horses were among the sights of Scotland and Ireland: the line of trace horses at the foot of West Nile Street in Glasgow waiting to help lorries up the hill to High Street goods station; the procession of carts up Carlisle Road in Londonderry; the laden brewery lorries along Holyrood Road in Edinburgh. William McGonegall put them to verse:

> Twenty horses in a row
> Every one of Wordie & Co.

And an Aberdeen joke remembered today:

> Knock, Knock
> Who's there?
> Ena.
> Ena who?
> Ena Wordie's horses.

This is a play on the meaning of Ena, either a girl's name or in Aberdeenshire "one of". Wordie & Co. horses became part of Scottish folklore to the extent that, as Margaret Gray records, well-upholstered Dundonian ladies were credited with backsides like a Wordie horse.

Horses sold to Wordie & Co. were already broken to draught work but they would not be used to city traffic and city noise. The noise was greater than the city noise of today: there was no chance, says Mrs Crawford of Belfast, of dozing off in the school classroom. She was brought up in Londonderry, off the Foyle Road, in Alma Place where the Wordie stables were. Young horses were broken into traffic by being led, the carter driving and another man walking alongside with a six-foot leading rope. This would continue for a few weeks and the loads would be light, say four barrels of beer instead of nine. Alternatively a young horse would be put on trace horse work, to which he might return at the end of his career.

When horses were taken into service it was often, but not always, the practice to dock the tails, thought necessary in case they became entangled in the draught chains, and it was also the fashion. Docking was done by the vet, but the bleeding was stopped by the blacksmith with a hot iron. Since the Act of 1949 docking has been illegal in the United Kingdom.

Because Wordie & Co. operations were almost entirely urban, the horses were stabled throughout the year. Some horses at rural depots could be grazed, as at Fort George where Mr R. J. Ironside remembers the one horse kept there grazing on the village football pitch in spring and summer.

Whereas on farms time was spent catching horses before yoking up, urban stable work was organized to a schedule. At the height of their business in the nineteen-hundreds, it will be remembered, Wordie & Co. had possibly nearly three thousand horses spread over sixty or so depots in Scotland and twenty in Ireland. In the smaller places the stables were often by the railway station, as at Beauly in Inverness-shire, where John Chisholm worked during the Second World War. John is now dead, but his brother Duncan recalls that one of the horses was called Charlie and two lorries were in service there. An unfortunate memory for Duncan as a schoolboy is of a Wordie horse with a load of furniture dropping dead in front of the Bank of Scotland in Beauly.

At the other end of the scale, in Aberdeen, Belfast, Edinburgh and in Glasgow the stables sheltered up to two hundred horses apiece. Even as late as the nineteen-thirties there were a hundred or so at Rodger's Walk in Aberdeen, and about the same number of men, who, Norman Bruce says, "sang, swore and squabbled". Mr Bruce was taken on as a carter there in 1929 but after two years learnt to drive a motor; indeed, in 1937 he drove the first Karrier Bantam in Aberdeen.

Among the larger stables were Wordie's first in Glasgow, in Paul Street off Cathedral Street (now submerged under Strathclyde University), where eventually some two hundred horses lived. These bigger stables were multi-floored with covered ramps leading up from the yard. There were two stable floors at Rodger's Walk, Aberdeen, with stalls for sixty-four horses on the lower floor and ninety on the upper.

Horses were tethered in stalls by a halter whose rope passed through a ring, the other end being secured to a wooden ball, called a sinker in Northern Ireland. It was made of lignum vitae or bog oak, wood nearly petrified by centuries of immersion in bogland and immune from attack by woodworm. The sinker not only secured the halter but took up the slack between the halter and the ring so that the horse would not put a foreleg over the rope and maybe get cast or pulled down in his stall. During harnessing the halter was simply removed and stayed put. There were loose boxes for sick and injured horses, three at the Mid Stables in Dock Street, Dundee. Bedding at Fraserburgh was sawdust, says Raymond Eddie, but peat moss litter spread six inches deep was

A view of Arbroath in the first decade of this century. The Wordie stables here were in Bell Rock Lane, where masonry for the Bell Rock lighthouse had been prepared.

more general, for example at the big stables in West Street, Glasgow. It was delivered there from Paul Street in bales bound with wire and protected by battens or peat-sticks, which were good firewood. Deliveries were daily along with the feed, says Duncan McNeill, who was a horseshoer at West Street from 1939 to 1950, latterly foreman horseshoer under British Road Services. Straw was not generally used as bedding because of its bulk, which added to problems of manure disposal, and because of the vermin it harboured; the rats liked it for their nests.

Manure disposal was a problem. A hundred horses could produce about fifteen hundredweight nightly. Although smaller stables like Arbroath had a midden in a corner of the yard, the bigger ones had to organize regular disposal. Robert Fulton says Divis Street, Belfast, with in the nineteen-thirties seventy horses, produced four cart-loads a week, or about five tons. This was carted away by farmers, but before they came two bullocks were always brought in to trample it down and consolidate it.

Mrs Kathleen Mills, of Riddrie, Glasgow, is similarly informative on this subject. Like so many who are quoted in these pages, she comes from a great family of Wordie & Co. staff. Her father, Robert McIntyre, was a carter and a foreman with them at Paul Street and Calgary Street until nationalization, and her brother James a trace boy and carter until he transferred to the railways; she herself sewed and repaired haps or wagon sheets for a while. Her brother James has added his recollections, and between them they say the manure was wheeled and tipped down chutes to a lorry beneath; this vehicle was often iron floored and sided. Once loaded, the lorry went to a railway goods station and the manure was transferred to railway wagons for distribution to the farms of

Opposite page:
The Arbroath stables as they were in 1939, recalled by "Dod" Suttie and William Birse. They have also remembered the names of the carters and their jobs and many of the horses. By 1939 the first floor was empty, but there are some horses on the ramp to show how it was used.

Central and Lowland Scotland; for instance to the tomato growers of Lanarkshire with whom Wordie & Co. had a contract, as Duncan McNeill recalls. Mrs Mills adds that manure from Paul Street and Calgary Street went to Sighthill, from West Street to General Terminus, from Argyle Street to Stobcross. The cleaner sort, she says, went to Hyndland for Colonel William Wordie's roses. Manure sales became a substantial item of the company's revenue, from the £2 sale to J. Paterson on 31st October, 1860, to the £2,193-worth sold in 1925.

As a child William Birse of Arbroath used to haunt the stables there in Bell Rock Lane, so named because the masonry for the Bell Rock lighthouse was cut in a yard in the lane. Together with "Dod" Suttie, who drove Wordie's parcels van in Arbroath before graduating to a heavier horse and eventually to a motor lorry, he has drawn a detailed plan of the stables and included the names of the horses in each stall, or at least some of them, the names of all the carters, and their jobs. The sketch makes it all clear: the ten stalls on the ground floor, with about the same number upstairs, the three loose boxes in the yard, the covered wooden ramp to the upstairs stalls, the corn room with its rat-proof metal bins or kists in the corner, the water trough. The lorries were parked in the yard, and the shafts were always chained back to the platform so that they stuck up vertical.

Larger stables followed the same general pattern. Duncan McNeill has drawn West Street in Glasgow, where there were three floors. Round the yard on the ground floor was the covered parking for the vehicles standing on an earth floor, along with the office, the watchman's bothy and the blacksmith's shop. Covered concrete ramps led up to the first and second floors, both filled with stalls, including three large stalls on the first floor. Here too was the feed store, with a hoist rope for the sacks, and here the saddler's shop and the surgery. Chutes for the manure were at the head of the ramps, and there were water troughs in the yard and on each floor.

Rodger's Walk, Aberdeen, described by James Wilson, was yet more comprehensive. In his time it was a garage, too; the stable side held a granary, a hay shed, a general blacksmith's shop, a cartwright's shop, a horseshoeing shop, a paint shop, a sick bay of loose boxes for twelve horses, a peat moss litter store, an oil store, a saddler and the office. All these were on the ground floor, plus the stalls for sixty-four horses. Ninety more stalls were upstairs, reached by two ramps. There were feed stores and water troughs on each floor. The stalls measured about eight feet wide by ten feet long, big enough for a horse to lie down in. In Divis Street, Belfast, they faced each other with a six-foot alleyway between, all the floors being concrete.

A.	Three Loose Boxes for Sick Horses	B.	Corn Room
C.	Leading Horses down from Upstairs	D.	Harnessing Up
E.	Drinking Trough	F.	Emptying Dung onto Midden
G.	Ready for Yoking Up	H.	Yoking Up
I.	Off to Work	J.	Lorry Park

Stall	Horse	Carter	Task
1	None	Left empty	
2	Jock	Dave McGee	Parcel Van. Passenger Station
3	Roan	Dod Suttie	Parcel Van. Passenger Station
4	Jimmy	Arthur Law	Stableman & General Deliveries. Goods Station
5	Punch	Jim Forbes	General Deliveries. Goods Station
6	?	Chae Ford (Foreman)	General Deliveries & Organizer. Goods Station
7	Leeb	Dave Strachan	General Deliveries. Goods Station
8	?	Jim Cuthill	Sundries. Goods Station
9	?	Davie Forbes	General Deliveries. Goods Station
10	?	Davie Greenhow	Wagon Horse Shunting. Harbour & Goods Yard

E.W. PAGET-TOMLINSON

Opposite page:
*Rodger's Walk stables
and garage in Aberdeen
in the nineteen-thirties as
recalled by James H.
Wilson. This plan has
been prepared from the
1:500 Ordnance Survey
sheet, with Mr Wilson
filling in details of the
buildings. Crown
Copyright*

Below: *West Street
stables, Tradeston, on the
south side of Glasgow,
were big enough to take
180 horses on two floors,
but by the nineteen-
thirties only the first floor
was in use. This plan has
been prepared by Duncan
McNeil, who was
foreman horseshoer there
from 1939 to 1950. The
ramps were made of
concrete and roofed
against the weather, while
their floors were covered
with peat moss.*

George Philp joined Wordie & Co. in Dundee in 1928 as a stable boy and then drove a team, that is a pair of horses. He records in detail the work that was done in the big Mid Stables in Dock Street, Dundee, which in 1928 held 106 horses. There were eighty in the Joint Stables, also in Dock Street, and thirty-eight in the West Stables. Three blacksmiths, one hammerman and one horseshoer worked at the Mid Stables, with three cartwrights and an apprentice in the repair shop. The apprentice painted the vehicles, but a local signwriter came to do the lettering, see appendix two. The saddler mended harness for Arbroath and Carnoustie as well as Dundee.

It was Wordie policy to centralize trades and to centralize the preparation of feed. Robert Fulton, who was yard foreman at Divis Street, Belfast, from 1934 until he retired in 1979, recalls the men employed there during the nineteen-thirties: three cartwrights, four horseshoers, one painter, one blacksmith and his helper, one saddler, one mechanic and three men to cut hay into inch or inch-and-a-half lengths, bruise oats and kibble or crush maize, mix it up and send it to the outstations in Northern Ireland.

A feed mill in a big stables contained the machinery to cut hay, crush oats and bruise corn. In March, 1925, Wordie & Co. bought the horses, vehicles and contents of the stables at York Road, Belfast, when they took over the cartage of the London, Midland & Scottish Railway (Northern Counties Committee) in Northern Ireland. In the "chop house" were a corn bruiser, a turnip cutter, a chaff cutter for the hay, a grindstone and a gas engine to drive all this. A supply of belting oil indicates a lineshaft drive, and there

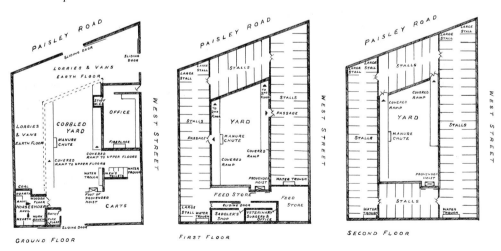

GROUND FLOOR

FIRST FLOOR

SECOND FLOOR

SCALE   0 5 10   20   30   40   50   60   70   80   90   100   FEET

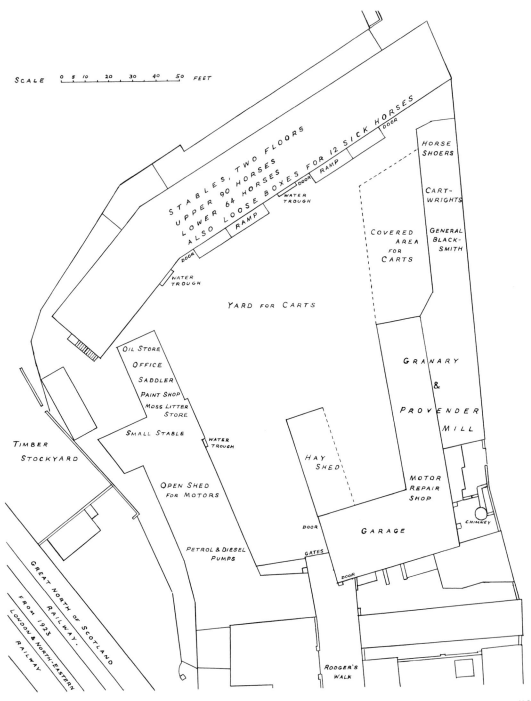

SCALE 0 5 10 20 30 40 50 FEET

STABLES, TWO FLOORS
UPPER 90 HORSES
LOWER 64 HORSES
ALSO LOOSE BOXES FOR 12 SICK HORSES

DOOR

RAMP

WATER TROUGH

DOOR

RAMP

DOOR

WATER TROUGH

DOOR

HORSE SHOERS

CART-WRIGHTS

GENERAL BLACK-SMITH

COVERED AREA FOR CARTS

YARD FOR CARTS

OIL STORE
OFFICE
SADDLER
PAINT SHOP
MOSS LITTER STORE
SMALL STABLE

WATER TROUGH

GRANARY
&
PROVENDER
MILL

TIMBER STOCKYARD

OPEN SHED FOR MOTORS

HAY SHED

MOTOR REPAIR SHOP

PETROL & DIESEL PUMPS

DOOR

GATES

GARAGE

CHIMNEY

DOOR

GREAT NORTH OF SCOTLAND RAILWAY.
FROM 1923
LONDON & NORTH-EASTERN RAILWAY

RODGER'S WALK

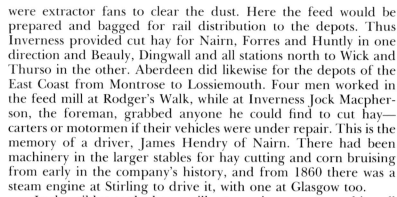

Fore shoes were more rounded than hind, both having welded-on toepieces for extra grip, while outside heels were thickened or staved up to compensate for the increased wear if the horse was a heavy wearer on the outside. The nail holes at the toe of the hind shoes were extra in case the hoof was broken, while the bigger square holes were for the frost studs or cogs. Note too the extra holes at the heel for rubbers if they were needed.

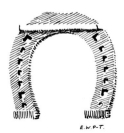

were extractor fans to clear the dust. Here the feed would be prepared and bagged for rail distribution to the depots. Thus Inverness provided cut hay for Nairn, Forres and Huntly in one direction and Beauly, Dingwall and all stations north to Wick and Thurso in the other. Aberdeen did likewise for the depots of the East Coast from Montrose to Lossiemouth. Four men worked in the feed mill at Rodger's Walk, while at Inverness Jock Macpherson, the foreman, grabbed anyone he could find to cut hay—carters or motormen if their vehicles were under repair. This is the memory of a driver, James Hendry of Nairn. There had been machinery in the larger stables for hay cutting and corn bruising from early in the company's history, and from 1860 there was a steam engine at Stirling to drive it, with one at Glasgow too.

In the wild state the horse will eat growing grass, munching all day, but the only means of supplying such bulk in an urban environment is by feeding hay, good quality summer hay with plenty of leaf and seed. In the earlier days hay was bought direct from local farmers; for example, in February, 1876, the Stirling stables bought £13 5s 6d worth from somebody called Menzies; this would be £13.27 in decimal coinage. Much bigger purchases are recorded: £92 odd in August, 1875, probably from a merchant. As the business expanded the bigger stables went for their supplies to merchants who would have bought from the farms, although John Wilson, now of Pitlochry, recalls his days at the family farm at Millerston near Glasgow. He has spoken of a Mr McCosh, a farmer near Lenzie, who sold Wordie & Co. 150 tons every year from 1920 to 1945. It was collected by Wordie's own motor lorries, which carried around 120 bales each, a bale weighing a hundredweight, so the total came to six tons. Some hay came from Canada in later days. Quantities consumed were considerable: the hundred horses in the Mid Stables in Dundee in the late nineteen-twenties would need five or so tons a week. No wonder everyone was pressed into service to cut it.

Energy was supplied by the bruised oats and kibbled or crushed maize, the bruising breaking open the husk, which helps chewing and digestion. Again large tonnages were bought and stored. An inventory taken on 1st January, 1858, of the feed stored at Glasgow includes 14 bolls of beans, 12 bolls of corn, 8 cwt of cut straw, 10 loads of hay, half a ton of turnips, 150 stones of uncut straw, a ton of bran and 12 bolls of barley. A boll is six imperial bushels; one bushel equals eight gallons, so a boll is forty-eight gallons. The costs were considerable: a hundred bolls of oats in 1860 added up to £106, and the grain account at Stirling for November, 1860, came to over £200, then a very large sum, say two year's wages for an office clerk. This would include all types of cereal. The bran mentioned above is the residue after the milling of wheat; it encourages chewing and therefore digestion, but was not given in such quantities as the oats and maize, although a bran mash made up with hot water was fed as a tonic, in Belfast once a week, or if the horse was chilled. Treacle was added to bran as an appetizer and a laxative. It remains in the memory of William Watson, who helped unofficially in the Falkirk stables as a boy in the late nineteen-thirties. He licked it off the back of his hand as he mixed it with the bran, which was put in a trough alongside the manger. Further interest to the food was provided by the occasional turnip, "once in a blue moon", Raymond Eddie says. William Wordie himself wrote to the *Stirling Observer* on 1st April, 1847, inviting farmers to grow carrots for horse feed. He said he fed his own horses on carrots with great success, and Robert Fulton remembers carrots on the menu at Divis Street in 1942, as they are at racehorse training stables and breeding studs to this day. To sum up: a horse would receive per day not less than 14 lb of hay, 12 lb of oats and 2 lb of kibbled maize, plus bran and treacle. The idea was to conceal the concentrated food, the oats, the maize, in the bulky hay, to make the horse chew more thoroughly and digest more effectively.

In the bigger stables the feed was loaded into trolleys and trundled up and down the alleyways between the stalls, each manger being filled in turn for the morning and evening feed. Otherwise the carter helped himself from the kist, scooping the feed into a box to take to the manger. For midday each horse had his sack and nosebag carried under the lorry, and often a pail too, although it was the practice to take horses to troughs for watering; they drank their fill at the stable yard troughs night and morning. If there was an epidemic, local authorities would seal up public troughs and pails had to be carried. The nosebags were canvas with wooden bottoms and could hold about 12 lb of chop. Strong in the

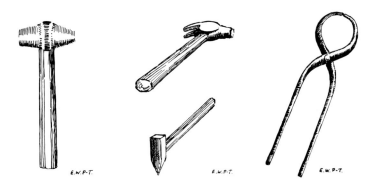

Left: *General purpose smith's hammer, weight 3 lb 14 oz, with a ten-inch shaft.*

Middle: *Light nailing hammer with claw for driving nails and twisting off the ends, weight twelve to fourteen ounces, and high tensile steel nail punch.*

Right: *Horseshoer's pliers or pincers for pulling off shoes and clinching nails.*

61

memories of many are the lines of horses at the goods stations solemnly chewing while the men went off for their dinner.

Shoeing was a never-ending task at a big stables. Working on granite setts or cassies the shoes would last only a couple of weeks, and never more than six. At West Street in Glasgow four horseshoers worked a nine-hour day as late as 1939 to keep the horses on their feet. Duncan McNeill was one of them; he recalls that they started at 6 am with half-hour breaks at 9 am and noon, finishing at 4 pm. Each man shod four horses between six and nine, two between nine and midday, while in the afternoon they made shoes for stock at the rate of three pairs an hour; pairs because fore and hind shoes are different, the fore rounded, the hind pointed. On Saturdays they worked from 6 am to 9 am, making a 48-hour week, and the pay was £3 9s (£3.45) for the week, modest even in those days. Note that the men were called not farriers but horseshoers.

Duncan McNeill adds details of the shoes. They were made from 1¼ by ½ or 1½ by ½ inch iron, with about one-inch heels and a toepiece welded on the front. For the winter each shoe had four square holes punched in it to take the steel frost studs, cogs or pikes which the carter carried in his box on the lorry along with a cogging hammer and his cover and ropes. He could fit them if road conditions demanded it. Sometimes rubber treads were fitted over the shoe for extra grip. Shoeing was done hot, which made for a more accurate fit.

West Street had a bricklayer and plasterer on the establishment to repair the stalls. His main task was relaying the floors, worn down by the constant stamping and scraping of hooves.

Iain McLullich contributes the atmosphere of the big Paul

Left: *Smith's anvils are multi-purpose tools: the tapered bic or beak is for shaping, the flat top behind the bic is of softer metal for cutting hot bar and other sections and the top face itself is of hardened metal with round and square holes for inserting shaping tools. Anvils were bracketed to a tree trunk with a central locating pin and pieces of cork at each corner as shock absorbers; it was these that made the anvil ring.*

Middle: *Jack for lifting axles, worked by a lever whose fulcrum could be varied by the range of pin holes. Once lifted the axle had to be held by packing, as the lever could not be secured.*

Right: *Wheel spanner for taking off the hub caps of vehicles; they came in many sizes.*

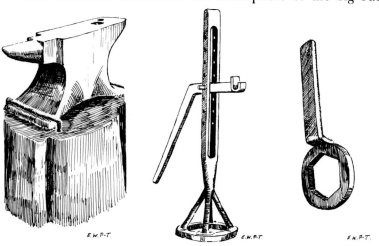

E.W.P-T.   E.W.P-T.   E.W.P-T.

Street stables in Glasgow in a poetic letter which must be quoted:

Seven-pound fore hammer for heavier work on the anvil.

The great blank wall occupying most of Paul Street had a doorway near the lower or North end. The first time I found myself there the smell from the opening attracted me, so I ambled into the doorway and stood there. Opposite was another long wall with a similar opening and a yard beyond.

To my right, against the wall and stretching apparently for ever was a line of square furnaces, each gleaming from blue to red and white in the centre of a heap of small coke. At each furnace was a short, squat, square man, capped and wearing a "brattie" or apron fronted by another large leather apron. Each was busy with bellows or tongs or hammer making horse shoes.

Amazed, I concentrated on the scene and watched and watched. I saw the nearest smith shouting over the background noise, not appreciating he was addressing me until he stopped work, straightened up, turned half round to face me and advised me my absence would be more appreciated than my presence . . . It was unfortunate that he was so forceful in that first encounter that he exhausted his probably limited vocabulary and so had nothing left but repetition for the many subsequent occasions.

Eh yes! There were many. Any time I could escape from parental captivity I was there, shoulder against the door jamb and head just peering into the interior until I was again given my congé.

The wall across from the furnaces was lined with stalls and here were the horses for shoeing. The smell of burning hoof was irresistible. Burning coke, red and white hot metal, hoof, stinking leather apron, sweat—euphoria! I can smell it still.

The frequent invitations to make myself scarce forced me to wander round the corner into Cathedral Street. Behold! Here was a great open yard. I watched a man, horse and cart enter, in that order. The man led the horse left and then round in a semi-circle. The horse was halted and backed until the cart almost touched the left-hand wall and was in line with the others already there. The horse was unyoked and the shafts raised to about vertical and chain-fastened. With trailing harness thrown over the saddle, the horse tramped over to the wall trough. Drink over, a slap on the rump and the horse made his way to the right-hand corner where, to my astonishment, he climbed a sloping stairway to the first storey, went through a doorway and disappeared left. Meanwhile the horseman had a crack with his friend before the two of them followed the second horse up the ramp.

I saw this repeated many times until one day, joy of joys, I too followed a horse up a ramp and turned left into an enormous stable lined on both sides with stalls. Thanks to one of those horsemen I saw the horse make its own way past empty and occupied stalls until it turned into its own and waited to be unharnessed. I was privileged to have the process explained to me by my mentor step by step as it happened and learned that saddle, collar, breechings, bridle, each had its own place at the stall.

That boy of four in 1912 had no words to describe "Wordie's"; seventy-eight years later he still hasn't.

E.W. P-T.

63

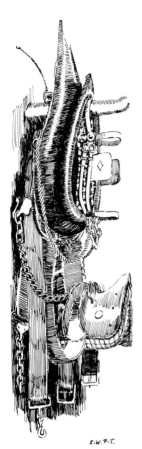

E.W.P-T.

Hung on the stall posts, the harness was ready to be put on in the right order.

Right: *A detailed study of the breechings, the collection of harness behind the saddle, comprising the crupper strap along the back ending in the dock or loop round the tail, the loin strap and behind it the hip strap, from both of which hangs the breech band.*

Morning for the horse started at 6 am with a feed, leaving plenty of time for digestion, and a groom. At a port like Belfast or Glasgow starting times could be earlier if a ship was catching the morning tide. The grooming was done by the carters and in the morning involved a thorough brushing, clearing the dandy brush every few strokes with the curry comb. The mane was combed down the right hand side, the tail was combed, and the leg feathers, while the hindquarters were washed to remove stains, and the eyes, lips and nostrils cleared with a damp cloth. Sometimes the mane and tail were plaited. Most important was a check of the feet; it was essential to have the soles clear of dirt. Evening grooming was lengthier: again brushing, wiping down with a cloth, clearing dirt out of the feet and maybe wisping down with a pad of straw, a kind of massage to tone up the muscles and prevent a chill. The work could take an hour after a day's cartage. At weekends the men took turns as "toun keeper", when they were responsible for "sorting" or tending all the horses; the term "toun" came from the farms (touns) where the practice started. The sorting included feeding, watering, grooming and mucking out, and the man was on duty on Saturday evening as well as all Sunday. Quite a few recall this, at Inverurie for instance, where the fathers of Mrs Mary Cassie and Miss L. Mitchell worked. Larger stables would need more than one toun keeper, unless stablemen were employed. At Divis Street, Belfast, Joe Galway says the work came round every six weeks and the pay in the nineteen-thirties was five shillings (25p) for the weekend.

Clipping was done once a year in October, trace high, that is about level with the shafts, to prevent excessive sweating when the winter coat came through. It was a good opportunity to clean up the legs at the same time, trimming the feathers.

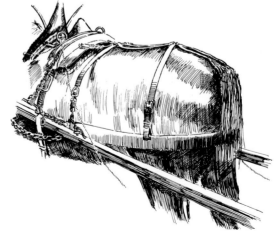

Harnessing was done in the stall, with the halter kept on until the collar and bridle were fitted. Sometimes the bridle was hung on one peg and the collar, hames, saddle and breechings on another. There could be two sets, light and heavy, the light for vans and light lorries, the heavy for box carts and the bigger lorries; the differences were in the type of saddle and the breechings, and in the collar.

First to go on was the saddle; not a riding saddle but the gear which carried the back chain, secured to the slide rods on the shafts and so supporting them, and in two-wheeled vehicles this would mean some of their weight too. The saddle was made up of the wooden frame or tree, padded underneath and covered on top by leather, with the bridge of the tree in which the back chain lay lined with metal. This was the channel which as described in Chapter one was kept well oiled to allow free movement of the chain as the shafts swung from side to side; the slide rods were oiled too, as the movement of the horse caused the chain hooks to slide back and forth. In Scotland this chain was called the rigwiddy or rigwoddy; in Ulster and elsewhere it was the back chain. In spite of this movement the saddle had to stay firm, otherwise the horse would have a sore back, so it was secured by a girth under the belly. Most often seen in Scotland was the Glasgow peaked saddle with an upswept front, a further feature being the two rings for the reins. This was a heavy harness saddle. The light saddle carried no back chain but a shaft strap, which was looped for the shafts to pass through; it did not necessarily have a peak.

Returning to the heavy harness, the back chain or rigwiddy could be adjusted to raise or lower the shafts, or trams; it was a good idea to lower them going uphill with a single-axle vehicle to throw more of the weight on the horse, the reverse downhill; in other words balance the load. The shafts were prevented from riding up by a belly band. Following the saddle in the harnessing sequence came the crupper to the tail and the loin and hip straps, all supporting the breech band, a wide piece of leather which went round the buttocks. Collectively this equipment was called the breechings and was designed for the horse to push against when backing, by sitting into the breech band; by the same token it would check a cart coming downhill. The breech band was held to the shafts by chains in the heavy harness and by leather in the light.

Now, with the halter removed, came the collar, by which the horse pulled. It was made from a straw pattern tailored to each horse, forming a ring shaped to the neck. Accurate fitting was essential, as it was on the collar that the shoulders pressed; an ill-fitting collar meant sore shoulders, so it was padded thickest where the shoulders touched but shaped to clear both withers and windpipe. In Scotland the high collar with a peak was often used on

To support the back chain or rigwiddy and therefore the trams or shafts, the heavy harness saddle was of substantial construction.

Below: *Light harness had a light saddle like a driving saddle, with a leather shaft strap which replaced the back chain.*

65

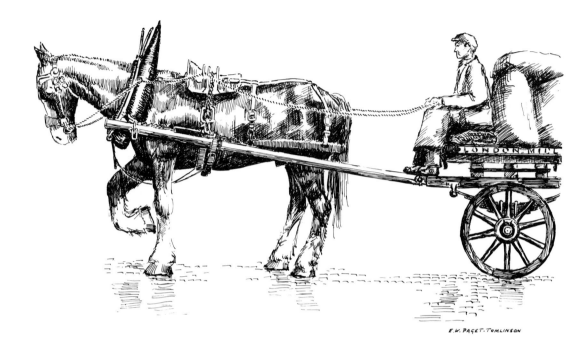

E.W. PAGET-TOMLINSON

Most used was the heavy shaft harness with a Scottish peaked collar and a peaked Glasgow saddle. In this picture the draught chains are hooked on to the shaft slide rods, but they could be taken to staples further back.

heavy single-shaft harness, called a Glasgow pike or a "tappit brecham" or a "peakit brecham". It spread to Ulster, too, although they had their distinctive pattern of opening collar which buckled up at the top, the straps being protected by a leather flap. Light harness had the non-peaked collar, also used by pairs or doubles. Their collar was the "dodie", as it was called in North-East Scotland. Because of its shape and the shape of the horse's neck the collar, unless it was an opening Ulster one, had to be put on upside down and then turned round. Enclosing the collar and next to go on were the hames, high and wide like horns on the peaked collar, more stunted "dodie hames" on the low collar.

William Birse says Wordie's hames and harness fittings were brass, others being polished steel. To the hames were attached the hooks for the draught chains, "drachts" in Aberdeenshire or "theats" in Glasgow, or trace chains. Because the hames were not secured to the collar but passed round it they could be rapidly released in an emergency by cutting the strap which bound their tops. If the horse choked, pressure could at once be taken off the collar, or if he stumbled his load was immediately released. Between the collar and the saddle there could be a light strap with a spring-loaded hook to stop the collar shifting, for the saddle with its girth was secure.

Next to go on was the bridle with bit and possibly blinkers, or in Scotland blinds. Wordie & Co. had both open bridles without blinkers and closed with them; there was some debate about the merits of blinds. Their purpose was to restrict vision to forwards and downwards, so that horses had less tendency to shy and would stand quieter. On the other hand with open vision they would tend to be less disturbed by what they saw. Bits varied: steady horses had a snaffle, the simplest type; difficult or nervous ones had a curb bit with a bar mouthpiece and a chain under the chin to check jaw movement, called a "watery chain" in Scotland. The snaffle was often detachable from the bridle and could be removed when the horse ate and drank. The bit went in first, then the bridle was passed over the head. Finally the reins, led from the bit through the rings on the hames and on the saddle.

Unharnessing was the same drill in reverse. Slipping off the cart, the carter dropped the reins over the hames and unhooked the draught chains off the cart, looping them and the traces to hang them on the hames on both sides. Next off were the

Left: *Head collar and halter, left hanging in the stall when the horse went out.*

Middle: *Low collars were called "dodies" in North-east Scotland and were used with light and heavy harness and with pairs. With them went low "dodie" hames, though the taller outswept hames associated with the peaked collar were often used with a low collar.*

Right: *Much used with heavy harness was the Scottish peaked collar or brecham, also called a tappit (crested) brecham or a Glasgow pike.*

E. W. P-T.

E.W.P-T.

E.W.P-T.

Three bridles: to the left the Scottish pattern of closed bridle with blinds or blinkers, in the centre the open bridle, to the right the standard closed bridle.

breechings chains, unhooked from the shafts, and finally the rigwiddy, the back chain. The shafts could be lifted clear as the horse was led away. The rigwiddy was refastened across them and they were pushed upright and chained back to the cart. Up at his stall the horse had his crupper unbuckled and the breechings swung off, followed by the saddle, girth and bellyband; all were hung on the harness rack at the end of the stall. The hames were now taken off the collar, the bridle slipped off and the collar gently turned and lifted off the neck, to be hung on the rack with the hames and the bridle, unless this was hung separately. The grooming brushes and cloths were hung on another peg and the horse's quarter cloth folded over the stall partition. Iain McLullich remembers all this as if it were yesterday.

The quarter or loin cloth was the horse's protective clothing; made of woollen cloth, it was designed to cover the kidneys in cold and wet weather. It was woven like a tartan in red and black check, with **WORDIE & CO** stencilled across in white.

So far this discussion has been about single-shaft harness, but Wordie & Co. had many pairs or teams of doubles for extra power, as a horse pulls more effectively when near the load. They were harnessed side by side to a central pole, for example in Dundee for the jute traffic, although they had been given up in Belfast from the early nineteen-thirties. Doubles wore low collars and "dodie" hames. From the hame hooks the draught chains led either to a swingle tree or direct to the vehicle. Harnessing to the pole was by a breast chain from each horse, secured to a metal D-ring at the bottom of the hames and passed through a ring at the front of the

E. W. P-T.

E. W. P-T.

E. W. P-T.

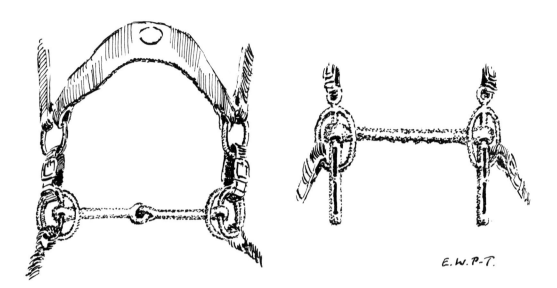

E. W. P-T.

pole and back to the D-ring. This way the horses guided the vehicle in unison. Breechings were retained for backing, assisted by the breast chains to the pole.

Cleaning harness was another job for the carter; many took bits of it home. Leather was washed and polished with boot polish; metalwork, buckles, hames and brasses were polished with Brasso and the chains burnished by a pad with lengths of fine chain stitched into it or by putting them in a sack of sawdust mixed with oil and paraffin and working them up and down—final polishing was by a soft leather cloth. Miss E. A. Fraser of Inverness remembers the children's task, holding the chains for father while he burnished with his chain pad.

Decoration was modest, except when the horses were on show; Wordie's kept a special pair in Glasgow for the shows, even sending them over to Belfast for the Balmoral Horse Show. Normally ornamental work was limited to a brass shape on the nose band and cheek strap of the bridle; if a martingale was worn between collar and girth, that was decorated too. But for shows it was different, with the full panoply of straps decorated with metalwork, fly head terrets which swung and flashed in the sun, ribbons and rosettes. There were many shows and parades in Scottish cities: in Dundee parades were held in aid of the hospital and lifeboat, while the Scottish Horse and Motormen's Association revived the Old Annual Horse Parade in Glasgow in 1904. Wordie horses won many trophies, and three of them remain in the family's possession.

Two bits, the two-ring snaffle on left and the Liverpool straight bit above. There was plenty of leverage on the snaffle if the reins were put through both rings, and on the Liverpool bit if the reins were taken to the straight cheekpieces.

69

Leith carters ready for a parade about 1910. The horse and lorry probably belonged to the Scottish Central Carting Co., but the turnout would be typical of Wordie & Co.
Photo Mrs E. M. Wood, who sent the picture from Australia.

Harnessed up, the horse was led down to the yard for yoking up to the lorry, and then away to work for the 7.30 am start at the goods station; often the lorries were kept at the goods stations and the horses would yoke up there. The carter would ride on the front near side of the lorry, sitting on his box or on the waggon cover until it was needed. None of these vehicles had seats or canopies and their leaf springs were harsh, so the carters wore the stoutest of protective clothing, as Raymond Eddie has described in Chapter one.

Horsemen and their Work   6

A S THE lorry rumbled over the cassies to the station the stable
staff went on with their mucking out, shovelling up the soiled
peat or sawdust and barrowing the manure to the chutes. At a big
stables like West Street in Glasgow the stable staff would consist of
two stablemen under a foreman, while at Rodger's Walk in
Aberdeen there were two men and a lad.

Fresh litter would then be put out and stalls, mangers and
troughs cleaned ready for the evening feed. Some carriers gave the
stable staff responsibility for grooming and horse care, but Wordie
& Co. made the carters look after their charges; they were not just
drivers. This way horse and carter were firmly bonded in trust, and
in revenue terms this probably paid off.

Longevity of service was a Wordie hallmark which has already
been demonstrated; here are more examples. Miss Mary Galway's
father was with Wordie & Co. in Belfast for fifty years and her
brother Joe for thirty-seven; in all five of the family worked for
Wordie's. Miss Eleanor Dickson of Newtonbreda, Belfast, has
written that her father, Ambrose Dickson, stayed for fifty-six years,
starting in Belfast as a message boy in 1909 when he was sixteen;
then he worked at Dundalk and Newry, where he became foreman,
and finally at Belfast. He retired in 1965 at seventy-two, Wordie &
Co. (Ulster) Ltd themselves finishing in 1972.

It was not the wages which kept employees with Wordie's, for
several correspondents admit to moving on after a couple of years
in search of something better; it must have been loyalty, although
correspondents are recalling times when few jobs were to be had
and it was prudent to stay put. But there is no doubt the men liked
the work and the former Ballymena and Belfast carter Adam
Gilmour sums it up well enough: "Wordie's were a great firm, great
bosses; if you were sacked from Wordie's you deserved sacking."

In Scotland Wordie & Co. were regarded with respect, as two
former members of staff at Inverness have said. William Munro
was a clerk in the office there in the late nineteen-twenties and has
commented how Wordie's as carriers were mainstays of the local
economy wherever they operated: "so many people and so many
businesses depended on them for their daily needs." R. J. Ironside,
who was a mechanic at Inverness just before the Second World
War, simply calls Wordie's "A Respected Institution".

There were plenty of characters among the carters, of whom

"Wordie's elephant" was one. This was Jock McFarlane, a cousin of Robert McNaughton, a Wordie carter in Stirling in the eighteen-eighties, whose daughter, Mrs Helen Bruce, tells of the "elephant", almost seven feet tall with hands like "square-mouthed shovels"; he could do the work of three men.

Eddie McCaffery of Edinburgh has written about George McDougall, who received a medal from the RSPCA and an award from Wordie & Co. for a particularly meritorious rescue. He was being loaded with butter from Gibson's shed in Leith Docks when his horse took fright and leaped into the water. Without hesitation George dived in; as well as keeping the beast's head up he completed the difficult task of unhitching the lorry and swimming to the steps that led out of the water. On reaching the top step the horse again shied and pulled George back into the water. He got it out at the second attempt. Such was the calibre of some of the staff, concludes Mr McCaffery.

More humorous were the recollections of Robert Fulton and Joe Galway of Belfast about "Yellow Jack" Ferrin, who shouted "Catch that dog, it's a parcel" as his lorry turned out of Grosvenor Street, a phrase picked up by the BBC; it is illustrative of the variety of Wordie's work. Another Belfast carter could neither read

Workers at Divis Street, Belfast, in 1936. In the back row, left to right, are: Ned McRory, painter; ?, horseshoer; Willie Mathers, mechanic. Front row, left to right: Willie Ovens, joiner; Joe Thomson, blacksmith; Robert Fulton, foreman; Johnny Mulvaney, horseshoer.
Robert Fulton

The Wordie (Ulster) football team. Veterinary surgeon Mr Roy Kirkpatrick recalls with Robert McClintock of Ballymena that one of the carters there in the late nineteen-thirties was Robert Blair, Irish Amateur goalkeeper, and the foreman was Davy Dunwoody, an expert on springer spaniels—in spite of the long hours they worked Wordie carters enjoyed their sports and hobbies.
Robert Fulton

nor write, but delivered correctly by recognition of the parcels once he had seen them placed in order on the lorry.

In modern eyes a carter's wage looks ludicrous. Fred Gunn joined Wordie & Co. as an office boy at Aberdeen in 1936 when he was seventeen, but became a statistics and wages clerk soon after. Following war service he moved to the Glasgow office, doing additional work as a collector of money from customers. In 1936, he says, an Aberdeen carter earned two pounds ten shillings (£2.50) a week; if he had a team of two horses he received an extra two shillings (10p), and there was by then some overtime, not necessarily paid by other cartage firms. In Northern Ireland the London, Midland & Scottish carters were paid National Union of Railwaymen rates in the mid-nineteen-twenties, higher than Wordie's, who in 1927 when they had taken over the LMS cartage in the province actually reduced carters' wages by two shillings (10p) a week. Some Wordie carters at the outstations were paid only twenty-five shillings (£1.25) a week, and that was before the reduction, but forty-four shillings (£2.20) was more usual, reduced to forty-two. Bear in mind again the considerable purchasing power of a pound in the nineteen-thirties.

Some carters were casually employed, like Peter Giffen, of Falkirk, who also worked for the rival Cowan & Co. and other carriers. Fred Gunn recalls one exceptionally honest casual carter in Aberdeen who found he had been overpaid ten shillings (50p) and returned the money, to the delight of the wages clerk, who would have had to make the amount up out of his own pocket.

So used was the horse to the way from the stables to the goods station that he needed few commands and no more than a touch of the reins. In Aberdeen it was, says Norman Bruce, "wish" to the

73

*To cut clinched-over nails to release an old shoe, and to knock out frost studs, the horseshoers made a special tool from an old rasp (**top**), the flat part being used for the former, the pointed part for the latter. Frost studs, cogs or pikes of high-tensile steel with tapered shanks were carried by carters on the lorry along with a cogging hammer (**bottom**) for knocking them in; its clawed end was used for taking them out.*

right and "hig" to the left, with "hip" to go forward, or maybe a click, click of the tongue was enough to start. Stopping was done by a check on the reins with the command "back", and backing by pulling up on the reins. Joe Galway and Adam Gilmour emphasize the lack of words of command, but the horse was constantly talked to, to maintain trust and confidence. Indeed a faithful horse could be called over from a distance, like Adam Gilmour's Jim at Ballymena, while James Hendry remembers "Cowboy" Morrison of Inverness who had his horse trained to come to him in the street as soon as he whistled. The horse was a big Clydesdale and he would come with his four-wheeled lorry to wherever "Cowboy" was standing, maybe many yards away, crossing the road and stopping alongside his master. Today it would be impossible in Inverness, but there was not much traffic in the nineteen-forties.

The short carter's whip with a two-foot handle and a two- to three-foot lash was used for signalling. At a right turn the carter had to climb over to the offside of the lorry to make his whip visible from behind, while if he had a high load he needed to stand up. Traffic moved slowly when all was horsedrawn, and photographs show the congestion in many a town and city. With the arrival of motors their speed was an additional hazard, and for that matter their not-so-effective brakes. Trams and their slippery tracks had long been obstacles to cartage, but the motor pushed its way in everywhere.

Noise of iron tyre on granite did no harm, but rain made the cassies slippery and horses would stumble, occasionally falling, and because of this knee caps were sometimes worn. If a leg was broken, the horse could only be destroyed. If the lorry overran the horse he could be pushed down, while a shaft might snap and the broken end gore a horse's flank.

Winter was especially hazardous, icy roads calling for frost studs on the shoes. Eddie McCaffery says they had to be put on each morning and taken off at night, otherwise the horse would be likely to cut itself in the stable. But in spite of the studs the horses still fell down, generally, as he says, in heavy traffic and between the tram lines. Insurance was taken out by the company and the carters had their own mutual insurance schemes, established for example by their union, the Scottish Horse and Motormen's Association. The company undertook the insurance of buildings, equipment and the horses themselves. Pension schemes were modest on the part both of the unions and the company.

Much has been said and written about the secret societies of horsemen, the Whisperers and the Society of the Horseman's Word, about their initiation ceremonies, their ritual, their inner knowledge, their use of special words. An excellent account of the apparently magical powers of some men over horses is given by

George Ewart Evans in *The Horse in the Furrow*, published by Faber & Faber in 1960. Ewart Evans discovered that men's control over horses did not depend on a word or a whisper but on a control of smell: a horse could be kept in his stall by coating the stall post with an obnoxious smell, while equally he could be charmed into docility by an attractive smell. The horseman would carry both around with him, but he would never reveal what went into them.

Many horsemen and carters would have had no dealings with such societies, although they had their weekly social meetings. The employers encouraged such gatherings, and, like the railway companies, themselves organized soirées, parades, outings and festivals such as the Edinburgh & Glasgow Railway Servants' Ball. Invitations survive of this, which appears to have been an annual event in October. Wordie & Co. were not behindhand in the organization of these affairs, their first annual soirée and concert in Glasgow being held in December, 1863. A report of one of these functions by a Dundee paper on 4th March, 1893, is typical. The occasion seems to have been a rather formal assembly, with Mr John Wordie in the chair giving what would nowadays be called a pep talk. However, dancing followed for several hours. Similar

Drawn from a nineteen-hundreds photograph, this illustration shows Wordie's carters on their way to the Woolmanhill horse trough in Aberdeen at the end of the day. The picture appeared in Andrew Cluer's Walking the Mat, past impressions of Aberdeen, *published in 1980.*
Drawn by kind permission of Mrs M. Winram, of Winram's Antiquarian Bookshop, Aberdeen.

Apart from rubber heels to give grip, some horses were provided with full or half rubber soles on both fore and hind shoes. This was intended as a protection if they had thrush, which is an irritation of the glands of the frog, or a corn in the sole. Treatment for thrush was to dress the sole with Archangel tar packed in with tow, the rubber sealing it in.

assemblies took place in Aberdeen, Falkirk and Glasgow, to foster loyalty and co-operation.

But to return to the secret societies; their existence was acknowledged and their initiation ceremonies known: for example the handshake with a hairy paw and the tying of a novitiate to a waggon wheel jacked clear of the ground and then spun so many revolutions.

Minor cuts and sores were dealt with by the carters, who had this responsibility too, although veterinary surgeons were called in if needed. The company had its own vet; Mr McFarlane, based at West Street, Glasgow, in the nineteen-thirties, is well remembered, and was well liked. Local practitioners were paid retainers, and in Dundee the vet would attend the stables daily, for, as George Philp says, Wordie & Co. had 224 horses in the city as late as the nineteen-thirties. Urban veterinary practice was then almost entirely horse work, with little interest taken in the small animals which occupy a vet today. Mr McFarlane himself went the rounds with the management on the yearly inspections of each depot, when not only the premises, horses and vehicles were looked at but also the condition of harness and halters.

The carters had some interesting remedies, making up their own ointments for sores and itches. Alexander Reiach was a carter with Wordie & Co. from 1929 to 1947, first having charge of a horse and lorry when still three months short of sixteen. For a while, from the age of twenty-two, he worked from Maud Junction, where the Peterhead and Fraserburgh lines leave the main Great North of Scotland route. It was here he found a cure for worms, at any rate to his own satisfaction. Worms, incidentally, were rarely picked up by urban stabled horses; they were more of a hazard to horses at grass. However, Mr Reiach had a young horse from Banff, very thin: returning from New Deer to Maud one Saturday morning he cut some broom from the roadside, chopped it into inch lengths and fed it to the horse over the weekend. Soon the horse was needing a larger collar.

He says a dab of Archangel tar was good for cuts and scratches in the summer, but an old ploughman gave this other cure: "urinate in a bottle, keep it for a fortnight and dab it on the cut". Colic, a digestive complaint, was treated by drenches given by a bottle. George Philp of Dundee describes how. A rope over a beam pulled the head up and a long metal medicine bottle was tipped into the mouth. After each small noggin the bottle was lowered to allow the horse to swallow and this would go on until it was empty. Any sign of the horse coughing would demand a quick lowering of the head and a pause until it was safe to proceed. Alternatively the head could be lifted and the mouth opened by applying a twitch, a rope passed round the upper lip and tightened by a long shaft.

E. W. P-T.

Grazed or sore shoulders could prevent a horse working, as he could not wear his collar. A remedy was to fit a special steel collar which would not bear on the affected part, or the saddler would take out some of the collar's horsehair stuffing and ease the pressure that way.

Epidemics were an ever-present threat. In 1947 at the very end of Wordie & Co.'s existence in Scotland there was a 'flu epidemic which hit the Belfast horses too. Belfast Corporation closed up all the horse troughs, while in Glasgow the Wordie motors which arrived one Monday morning from outside depots had to stay for the week to handle city deliveries. William Binnie from Dundee was one of the unfortunates, but in earlier years there had been more serious outbreaks.

Strangles was another disease which could reach epidemic proportions; it was spread, it was believed, by travelling folk. Mr McCaughey remembers an outbreak at Wordie's stables at Bally-mena in the nineteen-forties. Strangles is a contagious fever, a streptococcal infection of the nose, throat and sometimes the lungs. There is a swelling of the throat and neck; the abcess would either burst or it would have to be opened to release the pus. In the nineteen-forties treatment by sulphonamides was starting and the Ballymena horses were given their pills by a stomach tube, which had to be disinfected after each horse. After strangles convales-cence was slow, taking at least a month, and work would build up if the disease was widespread, as happened at Ballymena. One complication among others was a weakened heart; the horse would eventually recover, but Mr McCaughey recalls the hill on Bridge Street claiming one horse which may have been worked too soon.

Glasgow, Edinburgh, Dundee, Newcastle and Aberdeen are cities of steep hills, and to keep the loads moving up the hills trace horses waited at the foot to give assistance. In Leith and Edinburgh

Below: *Trace horses hitched their rope traces to the slide rods on the lorry shafts, which allowed easy release at the top of the hill.*

E.W. PAGET-TOMLINSON

trace horses helped on two routes. Eddie McCaffery was one of the trace boys in 1937 and he has described the work in detail. Generally trace horses were older animals, retired from the lorries to lighter work. Their harness was simple, a heavy collar and a bridle, a light leather back strap, and instead of draught chains they had ropes with hooks at each end. One hook went over the hame hook, the other on the long slide rod on the shafts. When a cart wanted help the trace horse went ahead and the boy hitched his ropes to the shafts, taking them off at the top. Coiling them up, he rode back to the bottom.

Eddie McCaffery, along with his mate, Bobby Rutherford, stood in Leith Walk above Pilrig. Their morning work was to help traffic up from Leith Docks which might go up to the top of Leith Street, round by the Post Office, over the North Bridge and into the High Street, or from Leith Street into Picardy Place, along Queen Street and into George Street. They started at 7.30 am but by dinner time the outwards docks traffic was easing off. So at 2.30 pm they moved to Holyrood Road to help the beer traffic from William Younger's. From here they worked up the Cowgate, but if the load were heavy they would go on to the Grassmarket and Lothian Road goods station. Work went on to 5.30 pm, then home at a trot to Jane Street stables in Leith. The horses were keen on this part. For a 52- or 54-hour week each boy earned eleven shillings and tenpence (59p).

In Aberdeen the trace horses stood in Guild Street goods station yard to help lorries up Market Street on to Union Street, the busiest route from the railway and the harbour. They were employed, too, up Marischal and Bridge Streets. An additional job for the tracers or tracey boys (the Aberdonians add "ey" to many words) was to straighten out the draught chains for the carters; they were given a shilling a week by each man they helped. This way the lads could add five to seven shillings to their wages, no more than 35p in decimal money but a fair sum in 1937.

In Newcastle up from the Quay the chain boys were helping with horses until the mid nineteen-thirties. Then a pusher tractor which also pulled was put to work; Cyril Yeoman, who was an office junior with Wordie & Co. in Newcastle for five years from 1931, thinks it was a Scammell. It was marshalled between two horse lorries. The big Newcastle carriers, Currie & Co., had two such tractors, as one of their staff, Edward Graham, remembers; James Hendry recalls seeing Karrier Cobs helping in West Nile Street in Glasgow in place of the trace horses. As soon as the cunning beasts felt the pull of a motor they hung back in the shafts. In Belfast trace horses were needed over the Albert Bridge across the Lagan because of its steepish approaches, but here as elsewhere point duty policemen were co-operative; they would wave on an

E.W.P-T.

approaching horse and lorry to give them a clear run over the bridge. At Ballymena trace horses stood at the bottom of Bridge Street to help the horses pulling drums of electrical cable up to the Northern Ireland Electricity Board depot from the station.

Best remembered were the trace horses at the foot of West Nile Street in Glasgow. Duncan McNeill says that in the nineteen-thirties there were generally five on duty and the boys would race home bareback every evening. There is a tradition that an elderly trace boy in the late nineteenth century, One-armed Bob, had lost his arm as a powder monkey at Trafalgar. Inverness had trace horses, but Miss E. A. Fraser says one man had charge of four; possibly the carters took them on to make up a team. Finally Eddie McCaffery saw the last trace horse in Edinburgh in 1947.

Behind the horse was the cart or lorry. Most of Wordie & Co.'s railway cartage was done by four-wheeled lorries of substantial oak construction, with a single horse in the shafts. Many were built for William Wordie by John Atkinson of Leeds, and in the eighteen-seventies they cost around £30. Atkinson seems to have been his principal builder, but he must have bought many locally. They were platform vehicles with the front pair of wheels on a swivelling forecarriage or turntable frame which allowed a turning circle of 23 feet compared with the 41 feet of a four-ton four-wheel motor lorry. Some builders gave a tilt to the forecarriage which gave the front wheels "toe-in", allowing a "castor" action which aided steering by helping the wheels to self-centre, a principle of steering early adopted by motors.

All wheels of the horse lorry had semi-elliptical leaf springs, and hanging ahead of each of the rear wheels was a skidpan or dragshoe which could be put under each wheel to lock it and so check descent. Once in Londonderry, Cecil Allen remembers, a skidpan slipped on the cassies coming down Distillery Road and the lorry overran the horse, which had to be destroyed; it was not a

Below: *Cousin to the standard lorry was the light one for local deliveries from country railway stations, the horse using light harness.*

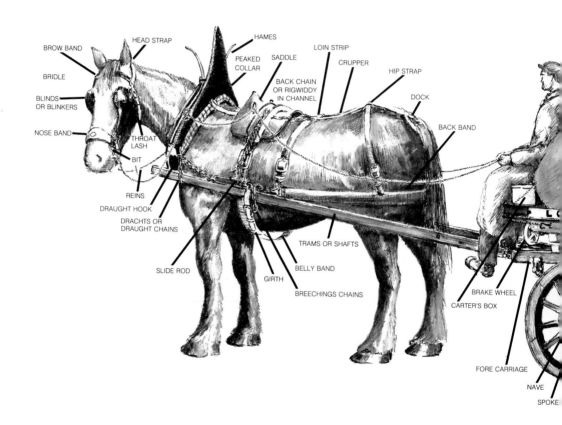

Wordie horse. Many vehicles, indeed most on railway work, also had iron brake blocks acting on the tyres of the rear wheels applied by a handwheel via a worm and nut linkage. They were essential in many cities, for instance in Dundee between the mills, the docks and the stations, and in steep-sided Glasgow.

Hanging under the platform along with the feed sack, nosebag and maybe a pail were a couple of skids for handling barrels. They were of six- by three-inch timber and about seven feet long, with cleats which fitted into slots at the rear of the platform. At the other end were wear plates. The lorry cover and securing ties, quarter cloth for the horse, cogging hammer and cogs or studs for icy roads were all kept in a box on or under the platform.

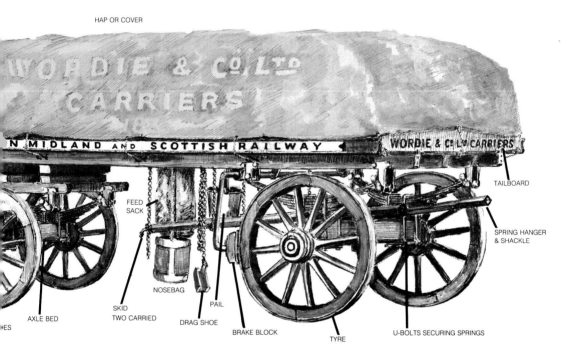

HAP OR COVER

N MIDLAND AND SCOTTISH RAILWAY   WORDIE & C?L? CARRIERS

TAILBOARD

SPRING HANGER
& SHACKLE

FEED
SACK

NOSEBAG

PAIL

SKID
TWO CARRIED

DRAG SHOE

AXLE BED

BRAKE BLOCK

TYRE

U-BOLTS SECURING SPRINGS

ES

The lorry cover went the length of the platform, and to cover the load was unrolled to its fullest extent and the four folds spread sideways. There were five securing ties each side, looped through eyelets or stitched to the cover and made fast to the hooks or rings under the platform. Railway covers had the eyelets with the four-foot ties made of some type of coconut fibre, generally nicknamed Glasgow Jock.

On brackets at each side of the forecarriage were enclosed candle lamps, the candles in spring-loaded holders which, apart from keeping them steady, pushed up the column of wax as the wick melted it away, an automatic feed mechanism. The side lamps had plain glass windows, the smaller rear lamp a red glass; the

A single-shafted horse lorry in Wordie's London, Midland & Scottish days, with heavy harness. The lorry was red throughout, with blue lettering, while the hap or cover was heavily treated with linseed oil, giving it a brownish sheen like an oilskin.

81

main purpose of the lamps was to mark the width of the vehicle and to protect its rear as the law required rather than to illuminate the route.

Single-horse lorries varied in length and width from 10 feet 6 inches by 5 feet to 18 feet by 7 feet. They could carry between two and a half and three tons, with a tare weight of fourteen hundredweight. Double or team lorries varied from 12 feet 9 inches to 18 feet in length; they could be more heavily loaded, to well over three tons. These capacities were adequate for the miscellaneous deliveries from a railway goods station, with the teams handling the heavier consignments, castings, crated machinery, steelwork and railway containers.

Some lorries had extra long shafts for overhanging loads such as tubes, shipyard plates, girders and rails. Normally shafts were about ten feet long, but these extra long shafts were eighteen, eight feet of the length being cross-braced for strength. They were heavy for a single horse, who could only manage them empty; laden they needed two or more horses in tandem, the leader with extra long draught chains to the shafts. There was generally a man to each horse. George Philp mentions a special low-bed horse lorry in Dundee that carried railway containers into Keiller's preserves factory, which had a low entrance door.

The float was a four-wheeler with a well, the rear axle being cranked. This was intended for crates of glass on edge, and sometimes steel plates for the shipyards; when the Royal Highland Show was held at Dundee it brought prize bulls from the station. For handling long shipyard plates, rails and timber there was the monkey, janker or pole wagon with a pole 24 feet or so in length; its rear axle could be positioned along the length of the pole of squared timber by means of a pin in a series of holes. A disadvantage of the monkey was its poor lock, limited to about a quarter of a turn. Both the float and the monkey were single shafted, but the monkey was generally drawn by two horses in tandem. For heavy loads such as castings and machinery there were low loaders with one-foot diameter wheels, and for really heavy loads like boilers there were two- or four-axle bogies, likewise with small wheels, drawn by as many horses as the weight needed. For theatrical scenery, light but awkward, a high-sided vehicle was used, needing only one horse.

Lighter railway delivery vehicles were called vans; they were four wheelers like the lorries but high sided, with the driver sitting well up on a high seat at the front. They could be drawn by a single shaft horse or by a pair harnessed to a pole. Lengths varied from eight to eleven feet and wheelbases from four foot five inches to seven feet. All had a good turning lock and the driver could keep control with a foot- or hand-worked brake on the rear wheels. But

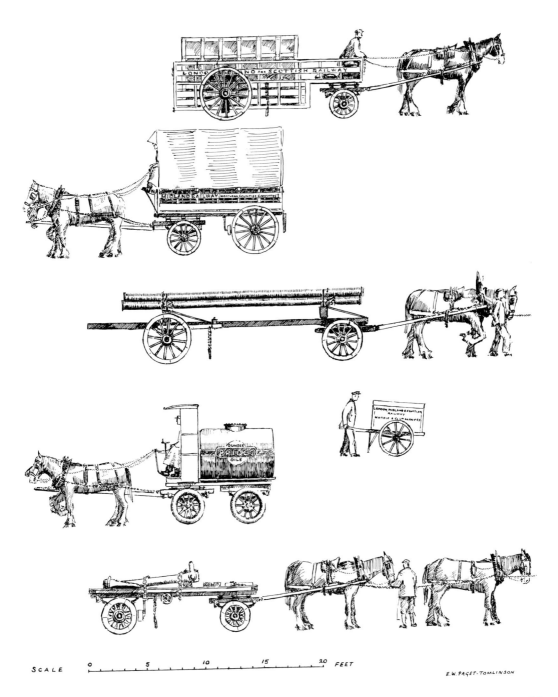

SCALE 0 5 10 15 20 FEET

E.W. PAGET-TOMLINSON

Below: For long loads extended eighteen-foot shafts could be fitted to the standard lorry; when loaded an extra horse or more would be needed as the shafts were so heavy.

he had to watch when backing in case the fore carriage went under the side of the van, which could scare the horse. The high sides allowed a mountain of parcels to be carried, protected by canvas covers or by a tilt. All these vehicles had to have their swivelling rings on the forecarriage well greased and their axles well packed with grease. There were no such refinements as ball or roller bearings.

Further down the scale were the two-wheeled high-sided coal carts with a tipping body, called in Scotland coup carts; these were also used in the sand traffic from the beach at Montrose recalled by Robin Pirie (see below). Alexander Reiach drove a sledge in winter from Maud Junction, a one-ton capacity cart with iron runners instead of wheels, ideal for wintry Aberdeenshire. With it he delivered locally and to New Deer, a village two and a half miles away, whence he returned to the station with eggs and trussed poultry. There were handcarts, too, for instance for local deliveries at Dingwall in Ross-shire, with the body boxed in to protect the goods from the weather, as remembered by Ian MacBean of Inverness.

In March, 1925, Wordie & Co. bought the horses, equipment and vehicles used by the Midland Railway (Northern Counties Committee) for cartage work in Belfast. Their fleet included eighty heavy four-wheeled lorries, eleven light ones, three monkeys or jankers, two four-wheel five-ton lorries and one ten-ton lorry and an assortment of parcels vans and floats, plus seven box carts, which were ordinary single-axle carts for coal or stone. Floats, or flat carts, were single axle too; these floats were for light goods, not the same as the four-wheeled glass floats. Seven two-ton "Derby" four-wheeled lorries are mentioned. These were made at the Midland Railway works at Derby and had steel naves to the wheels, which made them freer running; they had a capacity of thirteen hundredweight. Then there were two linen vans, not for the transport of linen, as might be supposed in Northern Ireland, but railway parcels vans of the London type with a covered tilt made of linen. One Ford van heralded the motor age.

SCALE   0   5   10   15   20   FEET

E.W. PAGET-TOMLINSON

84

Carrying the Goods 7

A T 7.30 am lorries were arriving at the railway goods station for the day's work. These varied much in size: at Inverness two railway tracks into a long goods shed with four more serving the yard, plus an end-on siding for loading vehicles and heavy material off a dock; at Fearn in Ross-shire a single-track goods shed.

On the lines north of Inverness it was possible for carts and lorries to drive on to the station platform and handle goods direct on and off a train. Larger stations had similar features, an overall roof sheltering a row of platforms or banks, one side of the bank having rail access, the other side road access; a normal arrangement was for the road to run as an avenue between two banks. The levels of the railway track, the bank and the road were so aligned that goods unloaded from a railway wagon could pass across the bank to the horse lorry or motor without the need to lift or lower. For heavy goods there were cranes, hand or hydraulic, often mounted at the foot of the station roof pillars. There were also lights for night work: oil lamps in the early days, gas and electric later.

The problem was congestion: a milling throng of horses and vehicles of all shapes and sizes trying to back and turn. Designed for horses, the stations had room only for horses; motors were unwelcome until Karrier and Scammell produced their mechanical horses, which had the same manoeuvrability as real horses.

Goods station offices were to one side or at one end of the building; additionally there might be huts on the banks or in the yard outside. Wordie & Co. favoured huts in the yard. The one at Waterloo Goods in Aberdeen still stands; it is wood and had a fireplace, a desk and a window. Other huts might be more substantial, built of brick or stone; Wordie's at Guild Street, Aberdeen, was stone. In them worked a clerk issuing waybills and collecting receipts and weight tickets; in and out was the foreman, hurrying on the work. In a small place like Nairn the foreman might drive the parcels lorry, a privilege reserved for himself, for it was not heavy work. Similar huts stood by the weighbridges, from whence the weight tickets were issued.

On railway work the variety of load was as diverse as one would expect when practically everything came by train. Provisions were a staple item, sent from the ports to the warehouses, from the warehouses to the wholesalers, from the wholesalers to the shops. Much of the traffic was in small consignments or "smalls" of one

Below: *Parcels delivery in towns was handled by vans with covers to protect the parcels; this is a small single-horse van.*

hundredweight or under, and as parcels; the latter were generally handled by a light lorry or a van with a tilt or cover drawn by a light-legged trotting vanner of 15.2 hands or so. He would do door-to-door deliveries and collections to and from private houses as well as shops and manufacturers, working up to three miles from the station. Each Wordie depot had its parcel lorry or van; Alexander Brechin of Aberdeen remembers it all:

I started in February, 1938, having been told to report to the office at the stables in Rodger's Walk. I was there at 7 am on the Monday morning to meet Mr Park, the boss at Aberdeen, and Jock Wilson, the foreman. I was so little the boss could not see me over the desk, so he told the foreman to take me over to the stable to meet my driver. He took me by the ear for about a hundred yards until we reached the stables, handed me over to my driver and told him what to do if I gave him any cheek.

I had to clean the harness and watch while the driver put it on so I would know how to do it myself later on, although I had to stand on a box to do it. I would help him to yoke the horse into the parcels van and off we would go to the railway station to fetch our load of deliveries. We had to sort them all out into different streets and I had to give the driver the parcels as he wanted them, so that they came off in the proper order. We delivered our morning load, which was over a big district; when we finished the driver took the horse and lorry back to the stables for lunchtime.

In the afternoon I had to go to the station to separate the parcels, as everything had been put on a big railway trolley. I had to pull the trolley outside and do the separating on the ground, ready for the driver coming back from lunch. When we finished our afternoon load we had to do collections from various factories and shops to take to the station, and then about five o'clock or sometimes later I was allowed home.

I cycled to work, so we loaded the bike on top of the parcels every day and if we had some for outlying districts I would tie them on my

back and on the carrier of the bike, saving the horse going to the outskirts of town. After I had delivered them I would meet the driver again somewhere along our route for some more to deliver. We worked from seven to five, Monday to Friday, seven to half past twelve on Saturday, for ten shillings a week, twopence being deducted for the stamp.

I was a van boy for two years and then I went on as a trace boy. We had to pull the lorries up the steep hills to the main street. Some days we had to go five or six miles when lorries were loaded with barrels of beer or when loaded with a furniture container. Sometimes in the afternoon I would harness my horse, yoke it up to a lorry and go round collecting bicycles from a few places and take them to the station. I was a tracer boy for only a year and then went on as a carter until I joined the Navy in 1942. When I returned in 1946 I was back as a carter for a couple of years. Under British Railways I went inside as a checker, ending up as a foreman after a few takeovers by National Carriers, Scottish Parcels, Lynx Carriers and the National Freight Corporation.

Occasionally Wordie & Co. sent lorries or carts to a small station which had no depot to handle the cartage. This happened at Auldearn near Nairn, Wordie's stable at Nairn dealing with the goods and parcels there. It was an all-day job for the carters, as Mrs C. M. Swarbrick, now of Stranraer, remembers, for her father John Allan was one of them. He would not return to Nairn until six in the evening. A lorry could manage in the normal way four delivery rounds a day from the station, two in the morning and two in the afternoon. Dinner was between noon and 1 pm at the goods station, the horses lined up with nosebags and pails of water. They never moved while the men were away. By 5 pm the last deliveries had been made, and the horses went back to the stables for a feed and a groom, but it would be towards 7 pm when the carter went home.

Although much of the traffic was delivery from the railway goods stations, the railway companies were equally dependent on their cartage agents for collection. In Edinburgh the beer traffic from William Younger's, McEwan's, Usher's, Edinburgh United, Steel Coulson, Archibald Campbell Hope and King, Jeffries, and Robert Younger was all-important. Edinburgh United and Steel Coulson had a single-horse Wordie lorry on full-time duty, Usher's had two, and at William Younger's in Holyrood Road there was a Wordie & Co. agent to organize the traffic. Other breweries were visited twice daily, morning and afternoon, by a Wordie representative, going the rounds in a trap.

In the nineteen-twenties that representative was John White, who recalls the intensity of the traffic. He had to telephone the foreman at Lothian Road goods station twice a day to tell him what was needed so that the right numbers of lorries could be sent up. Steel Coulson did a big export trade for the troops in India and

Hong Kong. Their casks bore an elephant symbol, and to ensure that the beer was disturbed as little as possible the elephant had to appear on his feet. Loads were nine barrels or six hogsheads for a single horse, fourteen barrels or twelve hogsheads for doubles (a team). Nine barrels weighed two tons; a barrel contained thirty-six gallons and a hogshead fifty-four.

Robin Pirie remembers that in Montrose Wordie lorries took the beer from the Lochside Brewery to the harbour for shipment to Newcastle, returning with empty casks offloaded from the coasting steamer. This is an example of the large amount of non-railway work which Wordie & Co. had built up. Wordie's indeed became known as the beer firm. In Newcastle, where Herbert Knox joined them as a Customs clerk in 1924, their main customer was Northern Clubs Federation Brewery Ltd, for whom Wordie's did all the local deliveries. Herbert Knox recalls that in Newcastle they also delivered for MacLay & Co., Steel Coulson again, Maclachlan's and others. Two lorries and drivers were on hire to Arthur Guinness Sons & Co.; the lorries were in Guinness colours and the men in Guinness uniform, with "derbies" or bowler hats.

There were also contracts with manufacturers such as the makers of Creamola, the cornflour substance of blancmange puddings, in Glasgow. The work was assigned to a lady carter whom Duncan McNeill remembers as Bella, the only lady carter at West Street. She took the Creamola round the shops with backloads of cornflour, finely ground maize, from the warehouses. By the nineteen-thirties female carters were rare, but in 1908 there had been eleven in Glasgow as opposed to 19,747 male. These figures are quoted in Angela Tuckett's book *The Scottish Carter*.

Running through the goods carried by Wordie & Co. one finds examples of work for mills, distilleries, merchants and shipowners, in addition to all the work for the railway. From Arran came barytes, a mineral used in the manufacture of paint which looked like crushed granite; it was brought into the Kingston Dock in the Campbeltown steamers, with whom Wordie & Co. had had a contract since 1888, and went to paint manufacturers in Glasgow. Nowadays barytes is used as a mud for stopping blowbacks in oil wells. Duncan McNeill says two lorries were on this work, and a further one met the crack Campbeltown steamer *Dalriada* to lift her Springbank whisky into bond. He also mentions the cartage done for Mirrlees Watson, the Glasgow engineers, who specialized in sugar refining machinery. Crated consignments were taken to the docks by one Johnny Wham, whose horse could travel through Glasgow on his own initiative, stopping at police-controlled crossings and moving to the policeman's signal; Johnny himself was regularly well oiled. Brewery work was more likely to encourage intoxication; William Birse once saw a driverless horse and cart come into the goods station yard at Arbroath, the driver slumped insensible among his barrels. Not only were the men rewarded with drinks and tips from certain customers but the horses too were "tipped" with a feed of oats, as Mr R. W. Kirkpatrick has discovered from talks with one of the Wordie carters at Ballymena, Mr Jackie Hogg. Naturally there was competition to deliver to these customers.

Because it was so competitive, cartage for the breweries was studded with allowances and rebates from the carriers. Thus on the examination of a rival weight ticket Cowan's were seen to be carrying William Younger's beer for two shillings (10p) a ton for the North British, although Younger's were paying only tenpence (4p) a ton. In other words, Cowan's were allowing Younger's one shilling and twopence (6p) on every ton as a rebate.

Similar allowances, generally well-kept trade secrets, were given for other traffics. To put Wordie's on an equal footing with Cowan's at Alloa in 1898, fourpence a ton (2p) was allowed to the British Dyewood and Chemical Company on all their collected and delivered traffic. This rebate was paid to the chemical company every six months by Wordie & Co., who reclaimed it from the Caledonian.

In 1927 the London, Midland & Scottish along with the other three companies of the grouping introduced road-to-rail containers as part of a campaign to gain business. At first the maximum capacity was four tons, but larger and smaller sizes followed, including an open design for bricks and insulated containers for meat and fruit. They were not a new idea; the earliest canals in England had had containers for the coal traffic, from the working face to the merchant's cart, and this was on the same principle. The railways benefited in their use by the increased powers of road operation they were granted in 1928, enabling them to carry containers by road throughout. They were found to be particularly useful for furniture removals and in Edinburgh the two biscuit makers, McVitie & Price and Weston's, employed them, Wordie & Co. taking them to Lothian Road.

Falkirk was the ironfounding centre of Scotland, dominated by the Carron Company. Large tonnages of coke, pig iron and moulding sand came by rail for road distribution to the foundries, or at least to those which did not have their own sidings. Out came baths, cisterns, guttering, downspouts, manholes and grids for nationwide delivery by rail, says Peter Giffen. Building materials were commonly carried by Wordie's, for instance bricks. Another Falkirk correspondent, Mrs M. Leishman, says they brought everything to build the Royal Infirmary in Falkirk, opened in 1931: stone, cement, sand, timber, slates, glass, pipes, sanitary ware, kitchen equipment, beds, mattresses, linen, theatre equipment,

Below: *Following the lead of the LMS in 1927 the four main line railway companies offered a road–rail container service for door-to-door deliveries, concentrating particularly on household removals, in which Wordie's participated.*

electric cable—it was a mammoth undertaking for horses. Horses too carried away the Falkirk tramlines when they were lifted in the nineteen-thirties.

Some traffic was seasonal, notably fish. June to September is the herring landing season at Fraserburgh, when more horses and men had to be sent up from Aberdeen, along with a clerk from the office. Ernest Simpson went there for five seasons in the early nineteen-thirties. Along with the herring came barrel staves for the Fraserburgh coopers from Sweden and Denmark. This was the period when German trawlers were landing large catches of Icelandic cod at Aberdeen; Norman Bruce says that for six weeks ten or twelve carters went to the fish dock when the auction finished at eight in the evening or later to shift the catch. Wordie's also handled the salmon netted at the mouth of the Nairn and the Findhorn; flat carts were sent along the beaches between Nairn and the Culbin Sands to collect the catch from the bothies. The season started in February so the work, which fell to the Nairn stables, was arduous, as Mrs Swarbrick says when recounting her father's experiences.

Aberdeenshire beef meant early starts, says William Lorimer of Turriff. There was in the nineteen-thirties a 6.40 am daily train

Nairn harbour at the time when the Wordie stables there was responsible for handling the salmon catch from the vicinity.

from Turriff to Aberdeen which loaded carcasses brought down from the slaughterhouse by Wordie & Co. horse lorries, four sides to a load. They were stowed in covered wagons, transferred to a London train at Aberdeen. Twenty-four hours later the beef, billed as fresh, would be on sale in London. The cheesecloths which had enveloped the carcasses were returned to be washed and re-used.

Mrs Mary Cassie of Inverurie and Miss L. Mitchell of Aberdeen had fathers who worked for Wordie's at Inverurie. There the station master checked with the slaughterhouse how many carcasses were to go, and Wordie & Co. took them, a ton of beef on each lorry, to the Smithfield train, which left between three and five in the morning. Again the cheesecloths were returned for scrubbing by local washerwomen in very hot water, using plenty of soft soap.

Turriff stables, incidentally, had to undertake some long-distance work in addition to the usual local deliveries. This was the transport of provisions to the coastal villages of Gardenstown, Gamrie and Pennan, the route to the latter depending on the tide; the descent to Gamrie was checked by a wooden sledge towed behind the cart. Return loads were dried fish, whiting.

Furniture removals, generally in demountable containers, were normal work from Beauly to Bonnybridge and included newly upholstered sofas and chairs to customers from the upholsterers of Kirkcudbright and Newton Stewart, delivered as Hugh Gray recalls by motor. Miss Eleanor Dickson of Belfast tells how Wordie's moved the furniture out of the LMS hotel at Portrush to Scotland.

The carriage of theatre scenery demanded a high-sided "monkey" long enough to take the light but unwieldy flats from the King's or the Lyceum in Edinburgh to Lothian Road. This was always Sunday work, after the last performance on Saturday evening but ready for the next billing on Monday. It was the same in Dundee and other cities. Another Edinburgh memory comes from John White, who recalls moving the Earl Haig memorial stone up to the Castle on a six-horse lorry, while Miss Mitchell tells of Wordie's moving the club house from one side of Inverurie golf course to the other.

Grain was always an important traffic; moving it in bulk was a lengthy business. As Jackie Hogg recalls, it took four single-horse vans two or three days to carry the weekly or possibly fortnightly consignment from Ballymena station to Morton's, the local flour millers. In the nineteen-thirties grain went out from Montrose harbour; by then collected from the farms by motor lorry, it was taken from the granaries to the docks by horse. Although the grain was bagged, each sack was opened at the ship's side and the contents were tipped into the hold, for the sacks were wanted again

E.W.P-T.

For long loads there was the monkey or janker, a type of pole wagon with bolsters over each axle for supporting pipes or poles. The rear axle was adjustable, being held by a pin which could be put in one of a series of holes.

E.W.P-T.

*Jute traffic in Dundee from the docks up to the mills was handled by either a single-horse lorry, which could carry eight or nine bales of raw jute (**above**), or by a pair, who could move fourteen to sixteen bales, a total weight of two and three-quarter tons (**opposite page**). Pairs were much used because of the hills; the driver sat on one of the bales so that he could see over the nearside horse.*

by the farmers; this process was known as "bleeding". Coal came into Montrose by sea and Wordie's took it to the merchants in two-wheeled tipping or coup carts. Timber, too, was imported. A local asset was fine sand from Montrose beach, collected by coup cart for use in locomotive sandboxes. Robin Pirie says the traffic had to be stopped for fear of erosion.

Dundee streets were dominated by the raw jute and flax traffic from the docks to the mills; George Philp has provided a detailed description. Because the way was uphill two-horse teams were generally used, an average load being fifteen bales at 400 lb a bale, totalling 2 tons 7 cwt. A single horse could manage eight bales. With eight, two bales were laid end to end on the lorry and five leant against them, the carter sitting on the sixth. With fourteen or sixteen bales three were laid down and the rest laid against them, except for the one used as a seat. Flax traffic was single-horse work because the mills were not so far uphill. Down from the flax mills came canvas bags and from the jute mills sacks of all sizes to the stations. In both World Wars sandbags were a priority, millions of them.

Parallel with the jute went flour from the docks to the bakeries of Dundee. In the nineteen-thirties it came in 140 lb bags, strictly half-bags; before 1914 full 280 lb bags had been used, "Hieland Mary's". Each two-horse team loaded sixty half-bags, 3 tons 2½ cwt; the carters had to carry them upstairs to the flour lofts above the bakeries, say twenty-two steps, where they were stored on their sides in tiers twelve bags high. For this extra work the carters were paid fourpence (2p) per ton every other Monday. Also in Dundee, Wordie & Co. had a contract to deliver rail-borne bread from the Bilsland bakery in Glasgow.

Another Dundee traffic involved special vehicles to take steel plates to the shipyards, latterly the Caledon yard. Short plates could go in a float, longer ones on either the long-shafted lorry or on the monkey, the vehicle with the adjustable rear axle described in Chapter six. Some plates were twenty-four feet long and would trail on the road, while long shafts made heavy work for the horses. Fortunately the route to the shipyards was level from both docks and station.

Granite quarrying and working was and is a major Aberdeen industry, and John McLaren has recorded much of its history. The working was done in the granite yards—there were ninety of them in 1914—making industrial rollers, fireplaces, balusters and tombstones. It was the job of the two main Aberdeen cartage firms, Wordie's and Mutter Howey's, to take the finished products, crated and straw packed, to the station for sending to the North of England, the Midlands and Wales and to the London boat of the Aberdeen Steam Navigation Company for London and the South.

The London boat sailed on Saturdays, and during the week both companies sent their representatives round the yards to discover how much worked granite was to be sent south. Wordie's representative was William Barron, with his bowler hat and bicycle. Each lorry could manage about 2½ tons downhill to the quay, but there was an uphill traffic, too, of imported Swedish granite in mixed blocks of up to nine feet by four for building work.

E. W. P-T.

Whisky had been an important traffic from the early days of Wordie & Co. It is thought, as said in Chapter three, that the company handled early consignments of Dewar's whisky in the eighteen-eighties; Dewar's had appointed a London agent in 1879, following up with a visit to London by T. R. Dewar in 1885. This, says the company, was their first attempt to capture a market in England, a London office opening in 1887. Wordie's also carried export whisky from Matthew Gloag's bonded warehouses in Perth and from the Rosebank distillery at Falkirk, while William Henderson of Dollar says his father worked exclusively on the cartage of Teacher's from the bonded warehouse to the docks in Glasgow, and Wordie's handled all Black & White traffic in the city.

In motor lorry days distillery work was much extended, many of the distilleries being remote from rail communication. Another traffic was in whisky samples, sent down to the Glasgow docks for shipment to Canada and the United States. They came, says Mr

Loading cased whisky for export at Matthew Gloag's new bond, Perth. P. J. Wordie

W. H. Hamp-Hamilton, from the distilleries in six- by six- by sixteen-inch boxes consigned to the Liquor Commissions at various places in the New World. Loaded on to a Wordie horse lorry and shielded only by a canvas cover, they were never tampered with on their way to the ship. Once aboard they were under the eye of the purser.

Theft, however, has always been a hazard for the road carrier. In December, 1837, four large Dunlop cheeses were stolen from William Wordie's premises in Stirling, while in 1850 the *Stirling Observer* reported two incidents. The first of these occurred in June when one Hugh Morrison pleaded not guilty to stealing half a hogshead of ale from a cart belonging to Forrester & Wordie while it was on its way from Alloa to Larbert station via the Forth ferry; he was found guilty and was given a month's imprisonment. Forrester & Wordie must have been another short-lived partnership like Wordie & McArthur. More severe was the punishment awarded to Robert Quare in October, 1850, for stealing hames and a martingale from William Wordie's stable at Alloa; because of his three previous convictions he was sentenced to seven years' transportation.

Wordie's Newcastle establishment handled the Breton onion traffic in North-East England. Herbert Knox describes how the onions and their sellers came by sailing ship to Newcastle, where Wordie's took the cargo to their Gibson Street stables for storage on the top floor. Here the sellers came to string the onions, and from here, Herbert Knox says, the Bretons sallied forth on bicycles to make deliveries.

How did Wordie & Co. earn their money on all this traffic? Their cartage business operated in two compartments: in one was their work as agents for the railway companies, in the other were their own customers, to whom they offered both cartage and storage facilities. Collection and delivery was their main work in both cases, but their system of rates and charges differed in each. With the railways they agreed tables of rates based on weight, so much per ton, the weight being that shown by the steelyard at the goods station weighbridge. The rates were broadly subdivided, a rate for general goods, a rate for bagged goods, a rate for parcels which went by parcels or passenger train, a rate for small consignments or "smalls" under one hundredweight, a rate for empties such as crates and barrels. Additionally there were categories of traffic known by their initials: C & D meant collected and delivered, the quoted rate being for the whole journey, parcels rates always being charged in this category; S to S meant station to station, the railway part of the journey, charged at lower rates since only part of the transit was covered—here collection and delivery was extra, or maybe undertaken by the sender and recipient; PLA meant passenger luggage in advance, when people sent their luggage ahead by passenger train to their holiday address or boarding school; there was also Through Bill traffic, which meant loads moving through one or more transit points.

The rates for empties were a constant source of complaint, but customers forgot they took up as much space as full containers and that they might be almost as heavy. Crates of empty bleach bottles, for instance, were no less trouble than crates of full ones. The calculation of rates per ton also took bulk into consideration.

Here are some examples from Northern Ireland, from Larne in 1926, when Wordie's took over cartage from the LMS: the general goods train rate for collection and delivery was two shillings and sixpence (12p) per ton, smalls for local collection and delivery twopence each (1p), threepence if going on or coming off the cross-channel steamer; returned empties were a penny halfpenny each, except for eggs and butter boxes which were a penny, all less than 1p in modern terms; for parcels by passenger train a penny halfpenny was charged for delivery.

Station to station rates by goods train were the same for general goods, two shillings and sixpence per ton, save for grain and feeding stuffs, one and six (7p) a ton. "Smalls" were a penny or so more expensive. By passenger train the general rate was three shillings (15p) a ton, and special rates were quoted for fruit and vegetables, for prams, motorcycles, tricycles, bicycles and dogs, all by passenger train. Other rates quoted in Northern Ireland were for pianos and organs by goods train, five shillings (25p) each; bath chairs by passenger train, one and sixpence (7p) each; theatrical scenery by goods train, four shillings (20p) a load during working hours, six shillings (30p) after working hours.

For their railway cartage Wordie & Co. charged the railway at these agreed rates. The evidence of their work was the weight tickets of the carters, details of which were entered in the office ledgers in this fashion: 4/3t 5 cwt, which meant four deliveries totalling 3 tons 5 hundredweight. At the end of each month the railway was sent an account for settlement, although the customers might be granted allowances and rebates as described earlier, which the railway might not know of. Thus in 1906 Wordie's allowed Steel Coulson, the Edinburgh brewers, a special rate of a shilling (5p) a ton, and to secure the bacon traffic to Newcastle off the Anchor Line ships in Glasgow Wordie & Co. had to give the same shilling a ton (5p) rebate as the North British contractor; this rebate was later increased to one and six (7p) as someone else was offering this. There were frequent arguments with the railways over the rates, already mentioned in Chapter four where Wordie & Co. were in dispute with the Great Northern in Belfast in the years before 1914. Wage increases meant rate increases, and it eventually became the practice, as R. J. Millar of Londonderry explained, to

E.W.P.T

Eighteen-foot-shafted lorries drawn by two horses carried plates from the railway goods station to the Dundee shipyards. The plates would overhang the platform at both ends, but more so at the rear; a too-great overhang at the front might foul the forecarriage.

add an agreed percentage on to the rates each year, ten per cent one year, five per cent the year after.

With private customers Wordie & Co. employed a rate structure based on tonnage and commodity. These rates were agreed between Wordie's and their customers, as Robin Pirie remembers at Montrose, where shipments of cement, coal and potatoes were handled. Rates to customers often included storage charges. Thus the Caledonian Milling Company of Aberdeen could arrange with Wordie's the storage and distribution of flour to city bakeries; Wordie & Co. would undertake to do this and send their bill to the milling company, who would pass on these charges to the bakers. With the Aberdeen fish traffic, the fish were taken from the auctions held in the evenings to the yards of the merchants or from one merchant to another; the merchant engaging the transport had to pay for it. It would go down in the account as 3-2s, 2-4s, the 2s and the 4s being stones of fish; three two-stone boxes for one merchant, two four-stone consignments for another.

Charges to Wordie's own customers in the nineteen-twenties and thirties have been described by Herbert Knox. At Newcastle,

The one-horse lorry was a familiar sight in any Scottish street as it rattled over the cassies. This is Dalkeith, but it might have been any town in which Wordie's had a depot.

he says, Wordie's asked a storage rent of fivepence (2p) per ton per week, while porterage in and out of the warehouse was charged at seven and sixpence (37p) a ton. These were general goods rates; special rates were quoted for certain commodities. Deliveries were charged according to distance, say seven and sixpence per ton within Newcastle; one shilling (5p) was the minimum charge per delivery.

Regarding rates as a whole, Mr Tom Atkin, a leading figure in the road haulage industry, has commented that Wordie's sometimes tended to charge more than others, keeping to a railway-style rates structure which their competitors would undercut; the nineteen-thirties was not a time of much variation in charges, once the initial road competition frenzy of the decade after the 1914–18 War had died down. The railways' ability to fight back, after their increased powers to operate road services were granted in 1928, kept rates to a realistic level; indeed in Newcastle Wordie's were most competitive with their rivals, Currie & Co., likewise railway associated.

Taking money from customers was done by collectors from the local Wordie office who went round on foot, or in latter days took a bus if they had to go further afield. They also collected on behalf of other Wordie establishments; thus people in Glasgow who had received goods from Aberdeen or Dundee would pay the Glasgow collector, Dundee and Aberdeen being credited with these takings. Similarly payment for Glasgow's deliveries in Dundee would be collected there but credited to Glasgow. This practice became widespread in the motor lorry age when the company were running trunk road services. These collections were from their own customers; the collectors would also take money on behalf of the railway companies as agents, and during a day in the nineteen-thirties might pick up £80 to £100. There does not appear to have been theft, but embezzlement did occur.

Fred Gunn explains in detail how the collections were organized. They originated from the carters' waybills, which were checked every afternoon by clerks from the office who took turns to come round to the stables at 4.30 pm to enter up all the work the carters had done for the day, both for Wordie & Co.'s own customers and for the railways. In Aberdeen this would mean two nights a week each for the clerks, three of them attending the stables at any one time. They had to attend on Saturdays, too, until 3 pm at the stables; the Saturday duty, Fred Middleton recalls, came round every third week for each of them. During the week the clerks were busy at the stables until 7 pm or later, but there was no overtime.

The entries were made in charges books which the stable foreman brought round to the office the following morning; in the

Two sizes of flour bag were humped into bakeries by Wordie carters, the 280-lb "Hielan Mary" and the so-called "half bag" of 140 lb.

office a senior clerk consulted the register book and priced each job for Wordie's own customers, say a delivery of sugar to a grocer or paint to a decorator. Junior clerks copied the priced jobs on to each customer's account and also made up the railway ledgers where the rates were agreed. By noon the accounts were up to date for the previous day's work.

Armed with this information, the collectors could do their rounds, collecting both for Wordie's and if required for the railway, although other arrangements might have been made. R. J. Millar of Londonderry says that when goods for the railway were collected the consignor paid the railway via Wordie's, but when goods were delivered the consignee settled direct with the railway. In Aberdeen Alastair McRobb remembers that merchants put a board inscribed "Wordie" in their window to tell a passing cart to stop and take a package for the railway.

An Aberdeen example described by Fred Middleton will show how railway charges worked. Three crates of pharmaceutical goods were delivered one day from Waterloo goods station to Davidson the chemist in Palmerston Road. In the evening the carter gave in his waybill and weight ticket, details of which were copied then and there by a clerk into the charges book. The following morning with the charges book in the office the job was noted and the amount added to the railway account, agreement having been reached over the accuracy of the weight ticket with the steelyard operator at the railway goods yard weighbridge.

Returning now to Wordie's own customers, big firms like Lever Brothers or British Oxygen had a ledger account and collections were made on their cash day, say the 28th of each month, when settlement was made by cheque. Wholesalers and shops receiving regular consignments were visited weekly for settlement or, along with lesser customers, might be billed at the end of each calendar month. The Wordie offices described these as "petty accounts" and collection was made soon after the bills were sent out. Individual customers would pay on demand, although, as Fred Middleton says, there were some difficult ones who were downright hostile when the charge was more than they had bargained for.

Fred Middleton was an office boy and clerk at Aberdeen from 1927 to 1938 and did his share of collecting. As an office boy his tasks were varied: coal for the stoves had to be fetched daily from behind the stables, but more urgent was the collection from the railway station of mail from the Glasgow Head Office and other mail from the Head Post Office. This was the day's first duty at 8 am. The office boy also acted as telephone switchboard operator, but in those days there were few calls, most business being handled by letter, because everyone liked to have a record of what was said and there were no tape recorders. He would be expected to deliver local letters by hand, acting as a runner, as R. G. Ireland remembers at Leith—literally running, he says. Another task for the lad was taking the weight tickets to the railway goods clerk for checking at the weighbridge with the steelyard operator. At the end of the day, 6 pm or later, the signed outgoing mail, entered in the mail book, was taken to the Head Post Office—never pushed into a letter box—while mail for Glasgow was taken straight to the station for the mail train; it did not pass through Post Office hands as it was in effect internal mail. Sometimes the managers would not sign their letters until after 6 pm because they had been out, so the boy might not finish until 6.30 or 7 pm and then, says Mr Middleton, home, but out again at 7.30 pm to evening classes, book keeping and arithmetic for him and, for a while, French; shorthand and typing for the ladies. On Saturdays work continued

Light shaft harness for the smaller lorries was more akin to driving harness, with a light saddle and leather traces instead of draught chains. The shafts were held up by a leather shaft strap, not a back chain or rigwiddy, and the breechings were given a turn or two around the trams or shafts, being held by a staple, as there was no slide rod.

E. W. PAGET-TOMLINSON

Pairs or doubles or a team yoked to a central pole were needed for heavier loads such as bales of raw jute from the docks in Dundee. They were more effective than horses in line behind each other, because both were nearer the load. The breechings enabled the horses to back and check the lorry, while the reins were crossed from horse to horse so that the same pull could be exerted on each.

to 1 pm. Clerks going to the stables to check the waybills would be working later, while on Friday nights at Newcastle Herbert Knox went to pay the men at Gibson Street stables and would not leave until 7.30 pm. He recalls how often the carters finished wet through.

Wordie & Co. offices, like most in the earlier twentieth century, were rather basic. Mrs Mary Gillespie worked at the Dundee office from 1916 to 1924. It was at the foot of Union Street between Dundee (Tay Bridge) station and Dundee West, the Caledonian station, which was a terminus with the Caledonian goods yard behind it. There was no running water in the Wordie office and staff had to use the lavatories and washbasins of the Caledonian station. Mrs Gillespie, then Miss Robertson, was both shorthand typist and secretary to the manager, Mr Hugh Pollock. David, the office boy, looked after the two coal fires; the cashier was a Mr Johnson, never to be seen without his bowler hat. Mrs

E. W. PAGET-TOMLINSON

Gillespie's wage in 1916 was 15 shillings (75p) a week; by 1924 it had risen to 37/6d (£1.88). The working day was from 9 am to 5.30 pm, 9 to 12.30 on Saturdays, with two weeks' holiday, which seems quite generous for the period, although Christmas was then a working day in Scotland. There were only two rooms, Mr Pollock's, where she sat, and a general office. Both were uncarpeted. Mrs Gillespie's are the earliest living memories of a Wordie establishment, just beating those of Mr George Findlater, who started as a clerk at Aberdeen in December, 1917.

In the nineteen-thirties offices were still equipped with high flap-lidded desks and high stools, with the ledgers on shelves bounded by brass rails. There was electric light, but an antique feature was the copying press, called in Leith the "jelly". To copy a letter dampened tissues were laid over the typescript and pressed down by the screw, so forcing the impression through. It was claimed that six copies could be taken at once. The correspondence was then bound up into a ledger which was filed in a cabinet. Copying this way was not always successful, but carbon paper was not generally used in the early thirties. However, typewriters were available from the eighteen-seventies, although the ledgers were entered up by pen and ink and the company minutes written the same way. Receipts and dockets, R. G. Ireland says, what might be called ephemera, were spiked on to long rods, possibly one rod for a year, and remained to gather dust.

Fred Gunn remembers that suits had to be worn to work, even on Saturdays, and clerks had to have a hat. But once in the office clerks would exchange their suit jacket for an ink-stained, cigarette-burned "office jacket". His memories are of a disciplined organization, an aloof management and a stern chief clerk. Talking of smoking: Herbert Knox says it was not allowed at Newcastle until after 6 pm.

In 1936 the office staff at Schoolhill, Aberdeen, comprised the manager, Mr McCowan, the assistant manager, Mr Ebenezer Duncan, the cashier, Mr J. Russell, who later became manager, the assistant cashier, Miss C. Duncan, Ebenezer's sister, the chief clerk, Mr Thomson, four senior clerks, three accounts collectors—one of whom, Mr Ernest Simpson, has helped with this book—three junior clerks, two lady typists and the commercial representative, Mr William Barron, with his bicycle. Some customers would come to the office to settle their accounts, which at that time needed receipting with a twopenny stamp. Fred Middleton recalls an earlier cashier who refused stamps to customers he did not like the look of, saying that he was not a post office.

There were more clerical staff at the warehouses. At Bannermill in Aberdeen there was a warehouse-cum-office manager, two clerks, a foreman and four or five labourers, added to now and

Below: *Ironwork from Falkirk was among the goods unloaded at Forth Road goods depot in Newcastle.*

again when big shipments were due. Warehousing became an important element in Wordie business. Bannermill was a public warehouse, which means that goods were stored there on behalf of manufacturers from all over Britain and on behalf of wholesalers in the city. Deliveries were made as ordered by commercial travellers and by retailers, and the clerks had to keep details of these. Their stock books were expected to tally with the stock in the warehouse.

Bannermill had five floors, including the ground floor. On the upper ones were grain, flour and animal feed, on the lower boxed and tinned goods from such firms as Lever Brothers, Del Monte's fruits and Libby's tinned pineapple. In those days no dented tin ever went out on sale. Also on the ground floor was farm machinery from Ransomes, Sims & Jefferies of Ipswich, along with cops of binder twine. The steel chutes which spiralled down from top to bottom were beloved by the junior staff, who never used the stairs. For raising the grain sacks there were hand-worked block and tackle hoists; the lorries backed up under them with goods from the stations and the docks. Boxes and cartons were barrowed into the lower floors, and barrels and casks rolled.

While some of the firms who used the warehouse arranged their own cartage under the instructions of their commercial travellers, in other cases Wordie & Co. fetched and carried on their customers' behalf, charging them as described on pages 96–97; a third possibility was that local carriers might come in, for example, for grain which had come from abroad, while farmers would collect their own seed grain.

Cyril Yeoman and Herbert Knox have clear memories of the work at Wordie's Newcastle warehouse in Melbourne Street, built in 1927. It had a basement and three floors with chutes, electric hoists, a case elevator and a barrel elevator which brought barrels up from the basement to the loading dock. Wordie & Co. had established themselves at Newcastle in 1896 using an old ware-house in Broad Chare, and in 1904 won a cartage contract with the North Eastern Railway, but this did not survive the 1923 grouping. They had from the first represented the Caledonian Railway on Tyneside and kept this work on for the LMS. Cyril Yeoman describes the Wordie office under the arches at the entrance to Forth Road goods station, like everywhere in Newcastle a strong-hold of the North Eastern, for whom Mutter Howey in a nearby office were cartage agents. At Forth Road small hydraulic cranes unloaded ironwork from Falkirk, cisterns, bags of nuts and bolts, hogsheads of raspberries for the Sylvan jam factory (these would come from Strathmore), and crates of glass. He says there were only four or five wagons a day in the early nineteen-thirties. Far different was the activity in the Melbourne Street warehouse in the

The quayside at Newcastle, where Wordie & Co. built up a considerable business from 1896 onwards. Trace horses were used to help lorries up from the quays until the mid-thirties, when a motor tractor was brought into use.

East End of the city, where Wordie & Co. had built up a business independent of the railways. Mr Yeoman says:

All day long goods were being received into store on behalf of our many clients, and there were many outgoing deliveries by our transport for delivery all over the North-East of England and parts of the North-West, while local provisions firms collected their orders. Stored at Melbourne Street were large consignments of tinned goods, Del Monte fruit, Prince's preserved meats, along with Horlicks, Nestlé products, Quaker Oats, pearl barley, flour, Sun Maid raisins, glacé cherries, drums of edible oils, condensed milk of all brands, borax, while we distributed large quantities of Watson's and Hedley's soap products. The list is legion . . . much of the goods stored was shipped into Newcastle Quay from the Continent and Scandinavia, while consignments of tinned goods from California were transhipped from the Port of London. We prepared and carried out the Customs work and were involved with many shipping companies, the Cairn Line bringing bacon in six-hundredweight cases, Furness Withy tinned fruit from the United States, Hall Brothers of Newcastle various, the Tyne Tees Shipping Company transhipment from London and tinned milk from Holland, Coast Lines barley from Leith, the Aberdeen, Newcastle and Hull Steam Company goods from Scotland.

The bulk of this was stored by us on behalf of the firms concerned and was delivered by us in accordance with instructions from their agents, with whom we had a very good relationship. To give you an idea of the efficiency of Wordie & Co.: orders received up to 5 pm were loaded by the night shift (together with anything collected during the day) and delivered the next day or at most the day after. On the driver's return the work was recorded in the journal by the late duty clerk, priced and invoiced the following day and posted straight out. No calculators or computers at that time.

Below: *Found at most Wordie depots was the coup or tip cart, used for coal, sand, gravel and bricks. Capacity was up to a ton, and tipping was so arranged that the cart body had to be lifted at the front before it went over, otherwise it might fly up out of control.*

At Belfast much of the cartage was from station to station and from steamer to railway station, involving short-term storage not only of goods but of animals. Robert Fulton says Wordie & Co. had not only to look after horses, which would present no problem, but also to care for donkeys, bulls, pigs, dogs and chickens.

One aspect of horse work remains: the hiring them out, along with lorries and carters. Sometimes all three were hired out to other contractors, as Robin Pirie remembers at Montrose. They could be paid by the day or the hour. In Glasgow the tobacco and cigarette makers Stephen Mitchell hired a high covered van and two grey horses to advertise their products; this was in the nineteen-twenties, says Mrs Kathleen Mills. In Dundee the whole equipage was hired out to certain of the jute and flax mills, the horses being stabled on mill premises. This was generally a yearly contract, but some firms such as the wholesale grocers Salmond & Fleming and the wholesale spice merchants Thomas Howden hired only the horse, again on an annual basis; these firms had their own vehicles and carters. Robert Fulton records that in Belfast during the nineteen-thirties Wordie & Co. hired horses to the New Northern Flax Spinning Company, to Messrs Arthur Guinness the brewers and to the bleachers Burt Marshall. These last had two Wordie horses and vans on a yearly contract, the vans being painted in their house livery.

Weaving jute depends on "batching-oil" to give strength and elasticity to the fibres. This came to the mills in horse-drawn tank waggons of 520 gallons or 2 tons 1 cwt capacity owned by the oil suppliers but drawn by horses hired, with their horsemen, from Wordie & Co. and others. Teams were usual; George Philp drove a Wordie team for six years on hire to the oil merchants William Briggs.

Shunting railway wagons called for a strong horse, and many

were used in Scotland and Ireland. Correspondents remember Wordie horses shunting at Ballymena, Fraserburgh, Inverurie, Arbroath harbour and many other places. At Coleraine work was done for the Harbour Commissioners, who took over from the LMS in 1926, the year the railway gave up their cartage commitments in the province. For harbour shunting Wordie's charged the Commissioners two shillings and sixpence (12p) per hour, £22 per month or £260 per year per horse. At Dundee seven or eight shunting horses were employed in 1939/40; William Binnie had charge of one of them. Called wagon horses, they used a variety of trace harness with a spreader or swingletree. Mr McCaughey explains that it was specialized work. The horse had to take the strain slowly, crouching down and exerting a steady pull. Once the wagon began to roll the horse stepped aside and left the shunter to control it with his pole, if necessary pinning down the brakes.

Wordie & Co. were not passenger carriers, but sometimes lorries were fitted with benches for school outings. At Portmahomack in Ross-shire Jack Mackay remembers how, round about 1914, the Wordie carter there took passengers to the train at Fearn, 10½ miles away. He charged a shilling (5p) for the single trip. Benches were put across the lorry, which was drawn by a pair. In 1934 a five-ton Albion came to Fearn and the horses left the Portmahomack stable, which was in the main street near the Carnegie Hall.

Before the motor age the horse made sound economic sense for journeys of up to eight miles, say a three to four mile radius from a railway goods station, which was their normal range of operation. For town deliveries within these limits they were unequalled, able to start, stop, turn and back in an instant. They were slow, certainly, but speed did not matter within such limits,

Above: *For light goods two-wheeled flat carts were sometimes adequate. Such vehicles were used to collect the salmon from the netters at the mouth of the Findhorn and take them to Nairn station. The horse wears light harness.*

Wordie's provided the railways and harbour authorities with horses for wagon shunting. The strongest animals in the stables, they had to crouch down and lean heavily into the collar to start a wagon rolling.

and if they had been faster they would not have been so manoeuvrable. Their disadvantage was their need for food and shelter; they had to be looked after rather than merely parked, and their feed became increasingly expensive. Further expenses were shoeing, harness repair and replacement, stable maintenance and, obviously, the wages of horsekeepers and foremen.

It was calculated by Wordie's in 1861 that a horse cost just over £100 a year to keep, a bit more in 1867, say £118. But in that year the company worked out a horse would earn £121. Some depots then did better than others: at Stirling a horse cost 7s 7d a day and earned 7s 9½d; at Stranraer a horse cost 6s 8d but earned only 5s 10d; and at Stonehaven cost 6s 8d but earned 9s 3½d. Twentieth-century balance sheets, for example 1925, show horse feed, stabling, shoeing and veterinary work, and wages adding up to £293,777 as against a total revenue of £394,501. So there was still some profit in the horse. In fact, as John Wilson of Pitlochry was told in the nineteen-thirties, if each horse made a profit of a few pence a week, that was all that Wordie's expected.

E.W. PAGET-TOMLINSON

Motor Transport 8

WORDIE & CO. ordered their first petrol motor vehicles in 1905 and 1906 for work in Glasgow and Aberdeen. The accounts of the period make no mention of their type, whether vans or platform lorries, nor of their manufacturer; it is not unlikely that they were made by the native Albion of Scotstoun, Glasgow, who had by 1903 developed a ten-hundredweight van. There seem to have been two in Aberdeen and possibly two in Glasgow; according to the accounts these latter were costing more than they earned. The Aberdeen ones did better, showing that the horse now had a rival.

Another threat to the horse came from the steam wagon, well established by the nineteen-hundreds. Wordie & Co. are known to have had two Foden steamers at Aberdeen and one at Newcastle, the latter on brewery work, for which the power of steam to move heavy loads from standstill was well suited. The R. Grierson subsidiary ran a transverse-boilered Yorkshire from 1905 to 1910.

Steamers could offer simple, robust and reliable machinery and a relatively low fuel consumption, something like three hundredweights of coal or coke a day when coke was, before 1914, eightpence a hundredweight. It had been found in the Liverpool trials of 1899 that the steamer could work twice as fast as a horse, but it did not like the frequent starting and stopping involved in delivery work, which used a fair amount of steam; the steam engine showed up better on a steady run.

Eventually, says R. J. Ironside, two Foden steam wagons were converted to diesel, with Leyland Moose engines. Mr Ironside, from Ardersier near Fort George, came to Wordie & Co.'s Inverness depot as a motor mechanic in 1938. He joined the RAF in 1940 and returned to Wordie's in 1946, emigrating to South Africa the following year. In South Africa he pursued a successful career with General Motors. He says the argument was that the Foden chassis and wheels were good enough for further service and a conversion would be cheaper than buying a new motor. There was some trouble with the gearbox, forward gear resulting in backward travel and vice versa, but this was cured by fitting an auxiliary gearbox, which at high speed emitted a howl that could be heard for miles.

By 1914 the petrol-engined lorry was well established, and it was used with success during the 1914–18 War. It was by no means so reliable as the steam wagon but had the advantage, if without a

SCALE 0 5 10 15 20 FEET

E.N. PAGET-TOMLINSON

trailer, of needing a crew of only one, plus instant availability at the turn of the starting handle. Fuel consumption in a 1920 four-tonner was about seven miles to the gallon; petrol was then less than a shilling (5p) a gallon. Like the steam wagon, the motor could move fast without fatigue, the driver being the limiting factor, but unlike the steamer there needed to be no stops to clean and make up the fire and to lubricate.

Water stops were still necessary, not for a boiler but for a boiling radiator; overheating on long climbs and low-gear work was a problem with early motors, and radiators would have to be refilled twice between, say, Dumfries and Manchester, as Mr Tom Atkins remembers from personal experience. It was normal to carry cans of water. Capacities were small, from three to five tons, for the engines were low powered and the vehicles, with their solid tyres, suffered from poor roads, neglected during the railway age and still surfaced with waterbound macadam. Tar was introduced generally during the nineteen-twenties, although it had been tried as early as 1896 as a binding agent to lay the dust and create a firmer surface, the start of tarmacadam.

The motor came to stay. Its success in the war pointed to a peace-time role for the many surplus vehicles which could be driven by the many trained ex-servicemen. Their advantages of speed, availability, compactness and cheapness soon became apparent, allied to something the railways could not offer, a door-to-door service without transshipment. At a stroke the future of railway transport, and for that matter inland navigation and coastal goods transport, was threatened. The railways were scared, although puny Albions and Leylands of five tons capacity did not look a match for five-hundred-ton goods trains, hundred-ton barges or nine-hundred-ton coasters, and in 1928 the railway companies secured powers to operate road services. Bulk haulage by road did not seem much of a challenge, in spite of the introduction of hoppers by the mid-nineteen-thirties, but for miscellaneous work the advantages of road transport became clear. It was easier and cheaper to load whisky at a Banffshire distillery and carry it straight to Glasgow then to transship to rail and again from rail to road. It was this type of work that laid the foundations of the country's road haulage industry, much encouraged by the advent of the diesel, of which more later.

Tied as they were to the railways, Wordie & Co. could not set up an opposition road haulage business, but they did see the value of motors to ease delivery work. There were motors early on at Stirling, Aberdeen and Perth, where bigger loads were becoming common. George Findlater joined Wordie & Co.'s office in Aberdeen in December, 1917, as a clerk, not quite sixteen years old. On 1st April, 1946, he became their District Manager at Perth,

One of the Newcastle Fodens and her trailer on beer deliveries. No precise details of their careers have survived, but the Foden "overtype" with the engine on top of the boiler was in production from 1902 to about 1928.

In 1905 the Wordie subsidiary R. Grierson of Glasgow bought a Yorkshire steam wagon with its distinctive transverse boiler. This had been introduced in 1903, and the Leeds-built Yorkshire continued to be made until 1937.

Glasgow-built Albions were early members of the Wordie motor fleet. Evidence of precisely what Albions were used in the nineteen-twenties is lacking, but the A10 must have been among them; introduced in 1910 with chain drive and solid tyres and a capacity of three to four tons, the A10 had a 32 hp engine.

During the 1914–18 War Leyland built some five thousand or more lorries for military use, and on their release four thousand were reconditioned for civilian employment. Wordie's used them at Inverness, Perth and elsewhere. Many stayed in service for twenty years.

109

thereafter Group Manager for Wordie's and later for British Road Services. He remembers a seven-ton Leyland at Aberdeen along with the two Foden steamers, while in 1923 a 2½-ton Leyland was transferred to Perth from Dundee, which by 1924 had two motors.

These early vehicles were put on local delivery work from the railway up to a radius of three miles, as was the small Ford van which Wordie & Co. bought in 1925, along with sixty-two horses and assorted horse-drawn vehicles from the London, Midland & Scottish Railway in Belfast. One task for the early motors, says Peter Giffen, was bringing horse feed from the principal stables, where it was made up, to the other depots in the area, in this case from Stirling to Falkirk. As has been noted in Chapter five, Wordie motors collected hay from the Lenzie farm of Mr McCosh, an annual 150 tons. The railway contract would allow these journeys, well outside the delivery radius, since they were not for hire or reward.

Delivery of horse feed was not Wordie & Co.'s aim when they bought motor lorries, but the first acquisitions showed their shortcomings when put on the tortuous duties of urban work. They had a wider turning circle than a horse, while wear and tear on the engine, transmission and brakes was considerable because of the constant stopping and starting and the low gear work, all of which meant higher fuel consumption and greater cost. Even in 1930 the future of the horse looked secure.

That year, 1930, however, turned out to be a milestone in railway cartage history: it was the year Karrier Motors brought out their Cob mechanical horse. This was the kind of motor for which the railway cartage departments were clamouring, combining the manoeuvrability of the horse with the speed of the motor, yet not needing the constant servicing a horse demanded. The LMS had been experimenting already with a small articulated vehicle, but the Karrier Cob provided the right versatility.

Clayton & Company of Huddersfield had been founded in 1904 as makers of railway fog-signalling equipment and detonators, but before 1914 they had diversified into motor lorry production, calling their vehicle the Karrier. In 1920 the company re-formed as Karrier Motors Ltd, building thereafter an increasingly wide range of motors from dustcarts to a combined road–rail lorry and a bus to the same pattern. These last came out in 1930 along with the Cob, which was a variant of their Colt, a three-wheeled dustcart chassis.

The Cob, built at the request of the LMS, was a three-wheeled tractor with a coupling gear which would pick up horse lorries. At first this gear was hydraulic and lifted the lorry's front axle, but the hydraulic gear needed hand pumping. It was soon replaced by a pair of inclined channels up which ran a set of guiding wheels

Opposite page: *Three stages in the development of the mechanical horse. The early Cob, at this pioneer stage with three small wheels, can be seen at top. The first experiments were encouraging enough for Karrier to increase the size and power of the Cob, as seen in the middle picture, and the introduction of the Wolverton coupling provided instant automatic coupling and uncoupling. At bottom is the Karrier Bantam, a four-wheeler with better stability and adhesion than the Cob; introduced in 1936, it remained in production, with modifications, for some thirty years. The Cob had the BK coupling, with spring-loaded jaws.*

mounted under the front end of a purpose-built trailer which would stand up to the speed of the mechanical horse better than the horsedrawn variety. Parallel with the Karrier development was the work of Scammell Lorries of Watford, who brought out their Mechanical Horse in 1933, using an instantaneous coupling which Karriers also adopted. The railway cartage service now had motors which could turn within the length of their trailers, although there were problems of backing a trailer which the drivers had to master, the need to steer opposite to the intended direction. The great asset was having a detachable tractor which could bring in a trailer to be loaded and depart with a full one and vice versa. The more intensive use of trailers led to more being ordered, and there was a tendency for trailers to stand around waiting for a tractor. Horses could work this way, too, and railway horses did, but Wordie's do not seem to have tried anything but one lorry to one horse.

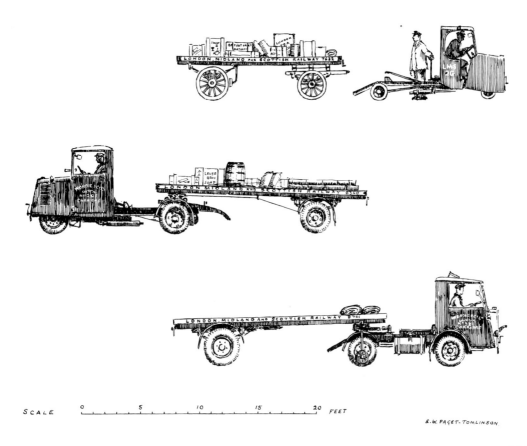

SCALE   0   5   10   15   20   FEET

S.W. PAGET-TOMLINSON

Wordie & Co. showed more interest in the Cob's 1936 successor, the four-wheeled 12 hp Bantam, which could also be bought as a rigid platform lorry of three to four tons capacity. The first Bantam tractor for Aberdeen was delivered in 1937 and was driven by Norman Bruce, who has contributed to these pages. A second Bantam arrived at Aberdeen in 1939, and by nationalization the depot there had eighteen Bantam tractors and sixty trailers, a good example of flexible operation. By swapping trailers a Bantam could manage two or three deliveries to a horse's one.

Inverness had Bantams, too, by the nineteen-forties, and some Cobs, the Karrier fleet there totalling a dozen or so, in the recollection of James Hendry. He says one disadvantage of the Cob was that it turned too tightly, with some danger of toppling over and bringing the trailer with it; tight manoeuvrability had at first been seen as a major asset. Another fault was the poor adhesion of a single front wheel, which created steering problems on wet or icy surfaces. The Bantam was an improvement, but the faults were not entirely cured. Trailer capacity was up to five tons. In Inverness the Karrier vehicles were painted a darkish green with yellow letters, not the Wordie dark blue.

The change from carter to motor driver was easy for some, the younger ones, but impossible for earlier generations. Mr Bruce had completed a couple of years as a carter when he was asked in 1931 if he would drive a motor. He spent one day under instruction, and the following morning was given No 11, a solid-tyred Leyland on local deliveries; then he had No 4, another Leyland with pneumatic tyres. He went on to the Bantam in 1937, and later taught others to drive them.

Normally the Bantam drew a five-ton trailer, but Norman Bruce recalls a seven-ton load, a boiler, from the Culter mills at Aberdeen to Invergowrie near Dundee, a distance of seventy miles.

He was not the only one to learn fast in the days before the driving test, instituted in 1935. William Binnie of Broughty Ferry was asked to drive on a Tuesday, started to learn the next day and was on his own the following Monday; that would be a risky business in modern traffic, but it was realistic in the nineteen-thirties. Others, however, as James Hendry says, never could accept motors and left; they could not understand the gears.

In 1928, to enable them to fight road competition, the railway companies were granted wider powers by Parliament to embark on road services throughout, and not merely as feeders to the rail services. This applied to goods and passenger work, and in 1929 air services were included. The new Act gave much impetus to Wordie & Co. motor transport, now able to go further afield on railway business without providing competition, save with a rival railway and with rival road haulage concerns. There was particular interest

CEREBOS SALT · SUNLIGHT SOAP · ROWNTREES YORK · ROWNTREES YORK · KELLER'S DUNDEE MARMALADE · MAZAWATTEE TEA · MAZAWATTEE TEA · CADBURY BOURNVILLE · CADBURY BOURNVILLE

E. W. PAGET-TOMLINSON

Following the Wolverton coupling Karrier introduced the BK, interchangeable with the Scammell design. Like the Wolverton the BK was dependent on guides on the tractor, leading a "spearhead" into a spring-loaded locking frame, the "spearhead" being integral with the sub-frame carrying the trailer's turntable and parking wheels. The trailer brakes were worked by a separate hand lever on the tractor, operating a push rod which passed through the "spearhead". There was also an independent parking brake worked from the trailer. To pick up a trailer the driver reversed his tractor under the former's front end until the "spearhead" engaged. To drop a trailer the driver released the locking frame and the "spearhead" dropped away.

on the railways' part to develop road services to country areas where there were no railways, and here Wordie & Co. participated to the full after 1932, when they came under London, Midland & Scottish control.

From this date they began to operate and develop long-distance or trunk road services, from Glasgow to Manchester and London, from Inverness to Glasgow and Wick (inherited from J. C. Brooke, a firm they took over), from Newcastle to the West Riding, as well as more local runs, from Dundee with jute to Kirriemuir, and from Montrose to Stonehaven. Drivers were given varied work, local and long distance. They never knew where they were going until they turned up for work, but they did not seem to mind this uncertainty; it added zest to life. The destination was marked on their waybills, headed by their names and vehicle registration numbers. There were known "digs" on the routes, and many drivers, says Rod Ironside, became family friends of their hosts. A modest subsistence allowance was paid by the company.

By the nineteen-thirties many makes of motor were available. Wordie & Co. to some extent standardized on the native Albion, on the Leyland and later on the diesel ERF, first produced in 1933. The Albion FT3 was a favourite, of five- to seven-ton capacity, with a fifteen-foot platform. Leyland Motors were by this time offering a wide range of motors of varied capacity, all named after animals: the four-ton four-cylinder petrol Badger and the six-cylinder petrol Bull, introduced in 1933, and the five-ton six-cylinder diesel Beaver of the same date. Lorries became bigger later, up to ten-ton capacity. Then there were six-cylinder diesel Bisons, Mooses, if such a plural is allowed, and Hippos, some of three- or four-axle design, which with their trailers could handle twenty tons.

For long loads such as pipes and poles a mechanical version of the monkey was employed. The forward part of the load rested on a bolster mounted on a turntable chained tightly to the platform, the rear part on a bolster carried on an axle of its own with twin wheels, to which it was also tightly chained. The load was the only link between the axles. This is an RAF type Leyland with a load of telegraph poles.

For long loads there were the motor equivalents of the horse-drawn monkey, also called monkeys, carrying pipes, poles and long timber baulks. Adam Gilmour described one working in Belfast: it was a rigid motor with a demountable bolster chained tightly to the platform, the bolster being able to turn radially. The load was secured to this, contained by a pair of upright stanchions; its protruding part was carried on a single or double axle bogie (the monkey), to which it was rack-chained, as the load was the only link between bogie and lorry. Tight corners and load overhang had to be considered when the monkey was being chained up to the load, and it was sometimes necessary to alter its position en route. A typical load would be three water pipes, totalling two tons ten hundredweight.

Robin H. Pirie remembers the motors at Montrose before the Second World War. There were four-ton Albions and six- to ten-ton Leylands which drew trailers of up to six tons capacity,

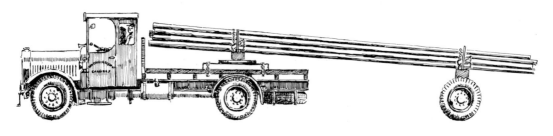

respectable loads, although the 1930 Road Traffic Act limited speeds to 16 mph on pneumatic tyres and 8 mph on solids when towing a trailer, if the motor's unladen weight was over 2½ tons. Cabs were primitive, with no glazed side windows, the drivers filling in the gap with cardboard and plywood. But they remained draughty, not much fun after a perspiring driver had loaded 120 bags of potatoes on his round of the farms. One cure was the daily paper thrust into every crevice, including where the controls came through the floor. For cattle transport between farm and auction

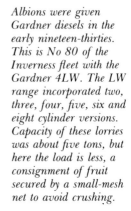

Albions were given Gardner diesels in the early nineteen-thirties. This is No 80 of the Inverness fleet with the Gardner 4LW. The LW range incorporated two, three, four, five, six and eight cylinder versions. Capacity of these lorries was about five tons, but here the load is less, a consignment of fruit secured by a small-mesh net to avoid crushing.

mart in Montrose the platform lorries were fitted with bodies or floats for the beasts. There were plenty of these at Inverness, two-decked for the sheep, Rod Ironside remembers.

Inverness was the main depot of the Highlands, with a District Manager responsible for Wordie outstations eastwards to Elgin and Huntly and northwards to Wick and Thurso, where in 1939 the resident driver was Charles Fairweather. By the nineteen-forties there was a substantial fleet of motors here, as two ex-Wordie Inverness drivers, Donald MacLennan and James Hendry, and the Inverness mechanic, Rod Ironside, all remember. Also with a good memory is D. A. Robertson, a near neighbour of Mr MacLennan at Dores, south-west of Inverness; he is the son of a road haulier who bought two former Wordie lorries when the Road Haulage Executive sold a large percentage of their fleet after the 1953 Act partially denationalized road transport.

Between them they have composed a comprehensive picture of the Inverness garage. Mr MacLennan, along with Dan Skinner, Charlie Innes and Alastair Ross, drove everything from petrol-engined General Service Leylands of 1914-18 War vintage, which Inverness had in the early days, to nineteen-forties diesel ERFs. They started their driving careers with J. C. Brooke & Co. of Inverness, who were taken over by Wordie's by 1938. The combined fleets included Leyland Beavers and Bulls and the two-ton Cub, introduced in 1930, as well as Albions, Bedford and

Austin tippers, while latterly there were a dozen or so Karrier Cobs and Bantams on town delivery for the LMS, while the District Manager was given a Morris Eight tourer driven by Rod Ironside which doubled as a breakdown utility. For a time James Hendry had a four-ton Albion, fleet number 138, with a four-cylinder Gardner diesel.

By the nineteen-thirties the value of the diesel was being recognized by road hauliers, and motor lorry manufacturers were offering a selection of engines for the heavier vehicles. Fuel economy was the main advantage, added to the sturdiness and reliability over long periods. There were none of the uncertainties of carburation of the petrol engine, which would in any case have become far too big and extravagant for the larger lorries being built by that time. There was, moreover, less fire risk with a diesel, while the Gardner range offered acccessibility for servicing and easy starting. The latter was by hand, with a decompression lever, dropped as the engine turned over. A heavy flywheel aided the starting, and two of the Inverness drivers could "swing the Gardner" without lifting the decompression lever. Wordie motors remained faithful to the starting handle almost throughout; in winter two men were often needed to turn it, one with a rope, and a good few wrists were broken.

Trailers were much used in road transport before and after the Second World War to increase payload. A second man looked after the trailer brakes, which at first were mechanical. The towing lorry is a Leyland Beaver, one of Leyland's extensive "animal" range, introduced from 1928, in this case a seven-ton diesel with forward control, where the driver sits ahead of or at least by the engine. Note the chains, a precaution should the tow bar or "stang" fail.

In the cab of one of James Hendry's other Albions the gear lever and handbrake were on the right-hand side, where there was no door, the spare wheel hanging here on the outside. A bulb horn and an electric horn were fitted; Wordie's had both in case the electric horn should fail. Reliable the Albion was, but slow. James Hendry, who was with Wordie's before nationalization and went on to drive for British Road Services, also has memories of the seven eight-ton Leyland Beavers, some with a "screamer" overdrive gear, while D. A. Robertson is knowledgeable on the Wordie Inverness fleet on the eve of nationalization.

By 1948, he says, the bulk of them were ERFs with AEC 7.7-litre six-cylinder diesel engines. There were seventeen ERFs, supplied initially to the Ministry of War Transport for carrying

munitions in France but acquired by Wordie & Co. in 1945/46. Although rated as seven-and-a-half to eight-tonners, they could carry eleven when a trailer was added, by now fitted with a vacuum brake. Then there were nine five-ton Albion FT3s with 4.25-litre petrol engines and one Albion CXIL with a four-cylinder Albion diesel. By this time there was only one Leyland, a seven-ton Badger with a six-cylinder 5.7-litre Leyland diesel. One of the ERFs was a tipper, and there were the two five-ton tippers that Donald MacLennan mentioned and the Bantams. Two more large Albions were in the fleet, possibly added on the takeover of another firm. They were ten-tonners with the 5LW Gardner diesel, the LW being built in a modular fashion to accommodate two, three, four, five, six or eight cylinders. They had three axles, two steering and one driving. Nicknamed "Chinese Sixes", these vehicles were developed in the nineteen-thirties.

By the late forties larger multi-axled lorries were coming into service, but the state of the roads forced weight limitations upon them, achieved by the plating regulations. These regulations ensured that vehicles were weighed and that the data were displayed on plates fixed to the lorries. The weight each axle could support was restricted, and to achieve a higher payload the third axle was moved forward. Ordinarily the six-wheeler had two driving axles with paired tyres and two differentials, a weighty assembly, but in the "Chinese Six" the third axle was steering only and tyre wear and weight was saved. An additional advantage was the siting of the rear axle well back, which allowed an even spread for a heavy load, avoiding too much weight on the steering. Makers were still offering "Chinese Sixes" into the nineteen-sixties. All the other lorries at Inverness were four wheelers, and most were registered there or in Ross-shire (the ex-Brooke lorries). This was not company policy; usually the motors were registered in Glasgow or Perth.

Driving brought problems, particularly at night when in the nineteen-thirties street lighting was minimal and the lamps on the vehicles feeble. Peter Giffen of Falkirk drove in those days of oil sidelights and one or two large carbide or acetylene headlights, with a single rear lamp which also lit the number plate. The acetylene was either produced in the lamp housing or, on larger commercial vehicles, by a gas generator on the running board or on brackets on the cab side; the carbide was carried in green tins. Much faith was placed in moonlight by the long-distance men.

Rain was dealt with either by wiping the windscreen with a cut potato or by the half-hearted efforts of a hand-worked windscreen wiper. An alternative to the hand-operated wiper was one which worked by vacuum from the inlet manifold; it would swish fast when the engine was idling, but would slow and even stop when the

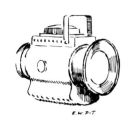

*Early motors had lamps burning Colza oil, a type of vegetable oil which the railways used (**upper drawing**). Carbide or acetylene lamps (**lower picture**) were also much in favour. The gas, generated by water dripping on lumps of calcium carbide, was piped to the burner. Earlier lamps generated the gas within their housing, but it became usual to have a separate gas generator on commercial vehicles with pipes to the lamps.*

E.W.P-T.

throttle was opened, just when most wanted on a steep hill. By 1936, however, electric wipers were available.

A single driving mirror was sited on the driver's side, so backing was hazardous; a driver had to ask a passer-by for help when backing alongside a pavement or into an entry. Nevertheless, by all accounts the morale of the drivers was high. It needed to be during the wartime blackout, when the sidelights were taped up so that only a hole the size of a sixpence remained and one headlight only was lit, the beam reduced by a frosted glass plate and a cover pierced by louvres. Hugh Gray explained how lorry drivers were at an advantage with this miserable illumination over car drivers because they were higher up and so could see the full range of the beam.

Excessive wear on the early pneumatic tyres in general use by the nineteen-thirties and weak springs were other problems for drivers and owners. The need for a second man when trailers were attached added to operating costs; this was a legal requirement, for the second man had to work the trailer brake. By modern standards road transport between the wars was slow; even in the nineteen-forties, James Hendry says, eleven hours were allowed for the 170 miles from Inverness to Airdrie, and twelve to Glasgow. There was a speed limit for lorries of 20 mph if over five tons unladen, and account had to be taken of the rest periods, more stringently enforced by the 1933 Road and Rail Traffic Act. Pitlochry was a popular halt on the run south from Inverness. It all sounds antiquated today, but given the road conditions of the time such speed limits were realistic.

In spite of their trials lorry drivers did not earn much more than their horse colleagues. James H. Wilson of Aberdeen recalls the wages structure which depended on the size of vehicle: up to two and a half tons a driver received £2 12s (£2.60) for a forty-eight hour week; over two and a half tons he was paid £3 1s (£3.05). If he had a trailer a driver received sixpence (2½p) a day extra. Overtime was paid at time and a quarter for the first eight hours and time and a half thereafter, the maximum week being sixty-six hours. An average wage with five hours' overtime would be £3 10s (£3.50), a pound more than was earned by a carter with a single horse.

Peter Giffen kindly lent a driver's handbook dated February, 1934; not a Wordie one, but from the rival Cowan & Co. stable, for whom he mostly worked. This is immaterial because the book is largely a quotation from the Road Traffic Act of 1930. It made rest periods obligatory, the first Act to do so. Five and a half hours' continuous driving was the maximum allowed, but in this time there had to be a half-hour break for rest and refreshment. Alternatively, the driver was limited to eleven hours' driving out of the twenty-four, or he had to have ten consecutive hours of rest in

Blackout regulations imposed during the Second World War demanded drastic lighting restrictions. Sidelights were taped up so that only about three-quarters of an inch of glass was clear, while headlights had their glasses replaced by frosted ones covered by a louvred mask.

the twenty-four. This last could be cut to nine hours in the twenty-four provided twelve hours' rest were taken in the next twenty-four hours, a rule inserted in case the driver could not take his ten hours' rest. The wording of the Act is difficult to unravel, but the overall picture remains one of long hours at the wheel, somewhat shortened by the 1933 Act. This brought in the log books, which it was the drivers' responsibility to keep correct. The rest of the handbook is taken up with speed and weight limits, reporting defects, what to do in accidents, what to do in the event of breakdowns, and drivers' responsibilities, to check lubrication and to wash the lorry. In emergency Cowan's Leyland drivers were expected to communicate with the nearest Leyland service station if they could not reach the Cowan office. Cowan's were, says Peter Giffen, "Leyland crazy".

Talking of accidents, William Binnie speaks of a bonus scheme the company had. For every three months clear of an accident the driver received fifteen shillings (75p) plus £1 15s (£1.75) at the end of the year if it was accident free. This could make him an extra £4 3s (£4.15) a year, but it was easily lost, because any accident told against it, whether the driver were guilty or not. A Dundee tram knocked off William's driving mirror, and that was the end of his bonus. Accidents were a constant problem for the maintenance men, as Rod Ironside recalls; most often they were minor ones caused by manoeuvring in awkward places or misjudging distances, but the repairs had to be made.

In the early days petrol-engined vehicles were serviced like the steamers by their drivers, who checked magneto contact breaker points, cleaned and reset spark plug gaps, lubricated chassis points, adjusted brakes and checked compression, but as fleets increased repair staff had to be recruited. James Wilson says there were four at Rodger's Walk, Aberdeen, before 1939. They could strip a motor down to the chassis and rebuild it if necessary. Service checks were carried out by one of the men every Sunday, and there were regular overhaul schedules.

James Hendry remembers three mechanics at Inverness in the nineteen-forties. They were Bob Mackie, Rod Ironside, and another who recited the ballads of Robert Service, so Rod Ironside recalls. With apprentice John Anderson they maintained twenty to thirty vehicles, but by that time there was only one cartwright to repair the dwindling fleet of horse lorries. Rod Ironside describes the rather simple workshop as just large enough to take one Leyland Badger, with a washdown on the apron in front, essential with cattle floats in use; petrol and diesel pumps stood nearby. At smaller depots such as Kirkcudbright, Hugh Gray remembers, drivers did the greasing and mended punctures, but for oil changes the lorries went to a garage in the town, Fairweather's.

Every two years of its life a Kirkcudbright lorry went to West Street in Glasgow for a major overhaul, if necessary a strip down and rebuild. It is possible that tyre maintenance was contracted out to the tyre companies, with a local representative checking pressures and condition, but no positive evidence has emerged. New tyres certainly came out to the depots from Glasgow.

Motors were garaged under cover alongside the horses. At Rodger's Walk, Aberdeen, the two Foden steamers went into open-fronted shelters facing an extension of the stable yard. Opposite was the motor garage and repair shop; petrol and diesel oil were stored in tanks at the yard entrance. In the repair shops pits had to be dug, although Wordie's were reputed to be against these. There were no pits at Inverness and work on a cold floor in winter was no picnic, says Rod Ironside. By the nineteen-sixties Wordie (Ulster) were putting in hydraulic ramps at Divis Street in Belfast.

Long-distance road haulage added further variety to the goods Wordie & Co. were handling in the nineteen-thirties and during the Second World War. The Brooke fleet acquisition gave Wordie & Co. their three-days-a-week service to Wick and Thurso, delivering to shops en route. Leaving Inverness at six in the morning the lorry, a five-ton Albion, would reach Bonar Bridge at 8 am and start its rounds, dropping off provisions (bananas are particularly remembered) from the Glasgow and Inverness whole-salers all the way north. The goods station and warehouse staff at Inverness knew where all the shops were and loaded in the right order, Bonar Bridge on the outside, Thurso in the middle. The Albion returned with milk, eggs, hides and skins and empty bottles in crates, for instance for the Parazone bleach works at Carntyne, Glasgow. At Inverness the goods were transferred to the Glasgow night trunk service. Both Donald MacLennan and James Hendry were on this north run, the latter recalling the loads of whalemeat from Scrabster to Melton Mowbray for the makers of Chappie dog food. A load was fifteen tons, chained down, the sides of the platform being built up to contain it. This was actually in British Road Services days, but the Wordie name remained in general usage into the nineteen-fifties.

Interspersed with the north run were more local jobs, such as margarine from the railway to the Coast Lines warehouse in Inverness harbour, from where it was distributed by Coast Lines' own road vehicles; barley grain to distilleries and flour to bakeries was a constant traffic. Donald MacLennan remembers curious loads like granite gravestones from Aberdeen to Dingwall and Wick. His most precious were soft fruits, skips of strawberries and raspberries, and boxes of tomatoes; they could not be covered by the usual tarpaulin, and instead a light small-mesh net had to be used to save crushing the fruit.

Opposite page:
Wordie's Inverness premises in the late nineteen-thirties, with an enlarged plan of the motor repair workshop. The yard was about a hundred square yards, the workshop about 27 feet by 11 feet, room for a Leyland Badger. Both drawings have been prepared by R. J. Ironside, who worked there. He remembers the workshop had no heating.

120

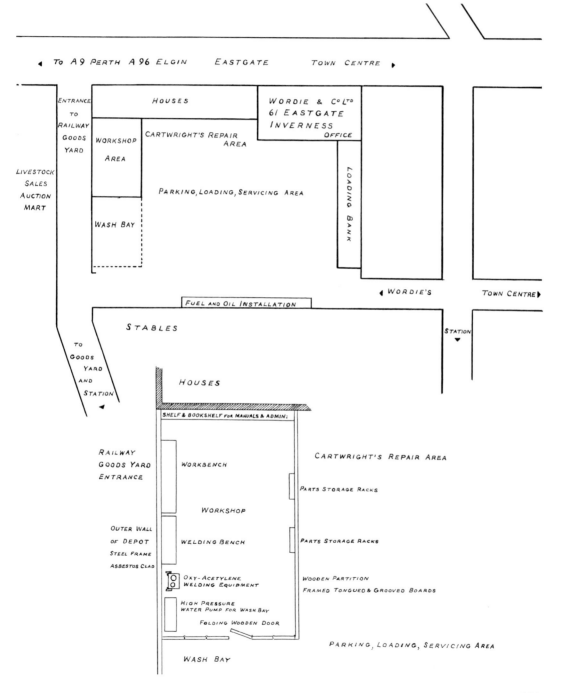

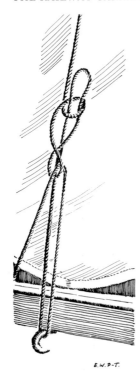

E.W.P-T.

The dwang: the bottom chain was held by a flat hook between the links, which were taken up on the point of the dwang as the chain was pulled down.

Wordie tarpaulins were pale in colour, remembers James Hendry, but stiff and heavy, with linseed oil as a waterproofing. This was essential as loads might stand overnight in heavy rain. Drivers learnt to build their loads up in the middle to form a ridge so that the water would run off, and to pass an extra rope round the load to tighten the securing ropes when they were wet. As many of these as possible were used, there being twelve hooks on each side of the platform, three or four across the back and one on either side of the heading board. Each cover or sheet measured twenty feet by fourteen, and a lorry would have three or four, since its platform could be twenty-two feet long and the load might be built up to eight feet. A good overlap was needed for weather protection.

Having unrolled and spread a cover, it was essential to secure it as quickly as possible, especially on a windy day, when another driver would have to help. Once one rope was over the others could follow, tightened by the carter's or driver's hitch, a variation of the sheepshank which could break a rope if pulled down too hard. Two ropes had to be passed round the back of the load and the covers had to be well down over the choke rail of the platform so that water could not drive up from below. Building a load was an art; a good driver was meticulous in checking his load, reroping if necessary if he had not supervised the building of it. He would come early for duty to do this, and would make further checks at regular intervals on the road.

Timber was held by chains tightened by a lever called a sylvester or dwang. Tree trunks were not so bad, but sawn timber is notoriously unstable and the chains had to be really tight.

Whisky butts or hogsheads had to be covered with two layers of sheets to hide them, although the smell betrayed them. They could be loaded upright or on their sides, held by chocks.

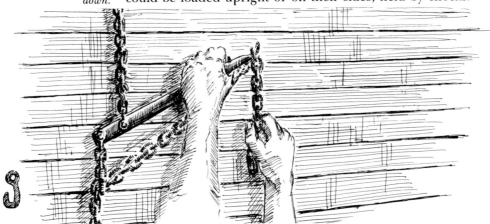

Wordie & Co.'s association with whisky goes back a long time, and distillery work became a major task for the motors. James Hendry recalls six lorry loads of whisky a week from Forres to Fort William in the nineteen-forties. The Inverness depot ran a three-days-a-week service to Glasgow on which export whisky figured prominently. Rod Ironside remembers the traffic in the summer of 1939 from the Millburn distillery in Inverness: the whisky was in sealed wooden hogsheads and Wordie's carried the loads straight through to Glasgow docks. He continues:

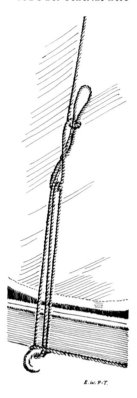

E. W. P-T.

> The sealed barrels were loaded inside the distillery in the bond area, under supervision of Excise Department officials, covered with "haps" (tarpaulins) and roped down. At 7 pm on the day of departure the driver and his trailerman collected the laden vehicles and proceeded direct, twelve hours including the Pitlochry stop.
>
> The run was not without incident. A Leyland Beaver with its trailer southbound for Glasgow ran too close to the edge of the drainage ditch just beyond Dalwhinnie at about 10.30 one evening. The sudden deceleration and the shock of impact loosened the load which moved forward, damaging the front load board and the rear of the cab. Two or three hogsheads of the ten on the platform turned on their bellies and stove in the ends of others so that gallons of whisky ran into the ditch and down the hill.
>
> Nearby was the Dalwhinnie distillery, and their Excise Officer was soon on the scene, verifying that the lost spirit "had not been consumed in the conventional manner", so that excise duty was avoided. But it was claimed that sheep downstream of the accident behaved strangely.

Inverness was also busy with barley to distilleries in North-east Scotland; it came up from Stirlingshire, too, in the Falkirk lorries, which in addition collected grain from Leith Docks. Grain was exported, too, from Montrose for example, the motors collecting it from the farms, the horse lorries shifting it from the town granaries to the ships.

Fish was taken by motor from West of Scotland ports to railway stations and to East Coast smokehouses, a major traffic being from non-rail-served Ullapool. Wordie & Co. handled milk collection throughout Scotland from Wick to Kirkcudbright, taking the churns from the farms to the stations or creameries. In Fife Mrs N. Gilliland remembers Wordie's coming to her father's farm during the nineteen-thirties, while Hugh Gray, who drove the Kirkcudbright milk lorry from 1938, continuing after nationalization with British Road Services, recalls the work clearly. Starting at 7 am, it took three and a half hours to collect a full load of 110 ten-gallon cans within a fifteen-mile radius of Kirkcudbright. By about half past ten he was unloading at the Stewartry Creamery in Kirkcudbright; for the rest of the day he went on general delivery work. During the Second World War loads of milk were going

Above and on opposite page: *Haps or wagon covers had to be roped down tight, and here the carter's hitch came to the rescue. Making use of the loop in the rope, a purchase could be made and a strong pull exerted, the end of the rope then being twisted round the hook and passed on to the next hook. From here it was thrown over the load and hitched on the opposite side. It was essential for the knot to be simple and easy to untie even if wet.*

123

straight to Glasgow to the big dairies, Ross's, East Kilbride, Clydebank Co-op. Mr Gray was doing 26,000 miles in six months. Parallel traffics were whey in 500-gallon tanks, two on each vehicle, from the Wigtownshire creameries to Tarff Creamery near Kirkcudbright, and cheese from Colfin near to Tarff. The milk cans were on two levels, ninety on the platform and thirty on a shorter upper deck. Short stanchions linked by chains kept them from falling off, and they were roped across and round the back as well. The big whey tanks were chained down. Once thirty-two ten-gallon cans were collected from a single farm, Cuil near Dumfries, a record.

Returning to Inverness, Wordie & Co. undertook transport of livestock by motor to the auction mart by the station goods yard. Rod Ironside recalls an occasion when a load of sheep were brought from the Kyle of Lochalsh in a float towing a trailer on which a demountable float had been mounted. The float on the lorry was longer than the platform and overhung the tail, which interfered with the trailer turning circle. Because of this the driver borrowed a longer stang or towbar, which altered the trailer following path.

All was well outwards to the Kyle, but on the return journey along the shores of Loch Duich the sharp curves close to the water at the eastern end of the loch spelt trouble for the trailer back end.

Butts of export whisky arriving from the distillery at Matthew Gloag's new bond in Perth, 1936.
P. J. Wordie

On a particularly sharp bend a rear trailer wheel cut the corner and
dropped into the water. As the trailer toppled the rear doors of the
float burst open and the sheep scrambled ashore without difficulty,
but recovering the trailer took three days; the lack of trees to serve
as anchors for block and tackle purchases posed a problem, solved
by using steel spikes. Another problem was accommodation for the
recovery team. Rod Ironside says:

> We were able to obtain lodgings with a widow lady who lived high on
> the western slopes of the Five Sisters of Kintail. The house was
> shrouded in mist morning and evening, was spartan in character and
> the meals more so. The abiding memories, other than the waist-deep-
> in-water struggle to put the trailer back on the road, are of stiff oatmeal
> porridge for breakfast and salt herrings at the evening meal, every day.

There were special loads. Norman Bruce had to winch a
Crimean War gun on to a Karrier Bantam trailer outside Gordon's
College in Aberdeen in 1940 for the scrap drive, while before the
war when the national grid was being expanded northwards
Wordie & Co. had made a speciality of carrying heavy electricity
cable drums on short wheelbase low loaders. At Inverness they
inherited this work from J. C. Brooke. The drums were delivered
to a strict shedule, loaded at Inverness station and taken to the site
where they were needed; the empties went back to Inverness

*Whisky en route from
Forres to Fort William
after the Second World
War. Six loads were
taken each week, ten
110-gallon butts making
up a load. The drivers
are Peter McDonald
(left) and James
Anderson (right).*
James Hendry

Bringing the electricity grid to the Highlands was a major undertaking in the nineteen-thirties and after the Second World War. Wordie's inherited some short-wheelbase cable drum transporters from J. C. Brooke, whom they took over by 1938. The drums were carried on steel A-frames and rolled off at the line-laying site; the transporters returned to the railway station with the empties.

station. At the line-laying site the full drums had to be transferred to the team's apparatus. In 1936 Wordie's took over the heavy hauliers Road Engines and Kerr, who with their steam traction engines handled complete railway locomotives from the Springburn and Queen Street, South Side, works of the North British Locomotive Company; they were taken to the big crane at Stobcross Quay for shipment. But this is another story covered in Chapter nine and in detail by others, as the bibliography shows.

At the other end of the scale were the parcels and small consignments vans, mainly Morris Commercials of varied capacity from fifteen to thirty hundredweight. They did urban work, for example mushrooms from the Great Northern Railway's goods station in Great Victoria Street, Belfast, to the Heysham steamers; in Londonderry they delivered Gallagher tobacco and cigarettes to the shops. Cecil Allen remembers one Derry driver, John Doherty, who had a terrier to guard his van; no consignments were ever lost.

Delivering from Beauly station, Inverness-shire, with a light lorry and light harness. With the driver, one of the railway staff, is John Chisholm, brother of Duncan Chisholm, who kindly supplied the photograph. John worked for Wordie's from 1939 to about 1945. The horse was Charlie.
Duncan Chisholm

In Newcastle Wordie & Co. had two 30 cwt Dodge vans which fetched and carried hampers between the station and the warehouse in Northumberland Road belonging to Pullar's, the dyers and cleaners.

Motor liveries were dark blue on the cab sides and red on the rear, a distinctive and unusual feature being the load plate screwed to the back of the cab. It said in large black letters LOAD NOT TO EXCEED 5 TONS, or whatever the maximum was. The company were firm about this, and William Binnie had to point it out when the Aberdeen foreman ordered him to load six tons of potatoes. Five tons said the plate, but the foreman never forgave him and picked him out for the poor jobs.

Photographs show vehicles with high fleet numbers like William Binnie's Albion 651. The later Wordie system was to number by make of vehicle. The Leylands were allotted the 200 range, the diesel Albions the 300s, the Karriers the 400s, although when they reached 500 they started again in the 400s as the older Karriers were scrapped; the 500 range was reserved for the ERFs and the 600s for the petrol-driven Albions. There was nothing hard and fast about this; the older lorries, whatever their make, kept their old numbers.

In 1938 the total Wordie motor fleet was 272, plus 113 trailers, and they still had 1,084 horses. In 1946 they had 380 motors and tractors, 220 trailers, 820 horses and twice as many horse-drawn vehicles.

Three Wordie mechanics at Divis Street, Belfast, with their Ford van.
Robert Fulton

127

From Grouping to Nationalization   9

IN 1923 Wordie & Co. were agents for new railways in Scotland, the London, Midland & Scottish and the London & North Eastern. Additionally they retained the work for the Burns steamers from Glasgow to Belfast and Dublin, from 1922 amalgamated with the Laird Line, who ran the Glasgow–Londonderry service, as Burns & Laird Lines.

Both G. & J. Burns and the Laird Line were under the overall control of Coast Lines of Liverpool, a group which in 1917 came within Lord Kylsant's Royal Mail empire and thereafter expanded fast, with the intention of dominating the regular coastal and short sea trades. Both Burns and the Laird Line had joined Coast Lines in 1920, the Laird Line having in 1908 acquired the Ayr Steam Shipping Company, who had run steamers between Ayr, Larne and Belfast and between Ayr and Dublin.

Steamer work was becoming important to Wordie & Co., particularly in Belfast. By the nineteen-thirties they were carting not only for the Burns & Laird Glasgow steamers but for their Ardrossan and Ayr sailings too; the Ardrossan service was one that G. & J. Burns had acquired in 1882. Among other companies which joined Coast Lines were the Antrim Line, the shipping division of the Antrim Iron Ore Company, in 1929 and, after the Second World War, the Belfast, Mersey & Manchester Steamship Company, which was a fusion of the Belfast & Mersey Steamship Company, with whom Wordie's had had a contract since 1897, J. J. Mack & Sons of Liverpool and the Belfast & Manchester Steamship Company. Wordie & Co. worked for both the Antrim ships and the Manchester steamers, along with the Glasgow and London sailings of the Clyde Shipping Company and the Bristol services of the Bristol Steam Navigation Company. An important contract gained in 1925 was the work in Belfast for the Heysham steamers formerly run by the Midland Railway from their new port near Morecambe, opened in 1904, for the Irish and Isle of Man trade. These had come under LMS control.

The contract was won because in 1923 the newly formed LMS decided to give up cartage work in Belfast for the railway they inherited from the Midland, work which included the Heysham steamers. The cartage work did not pay them, one possible reason being that their men were paid at National Union of Railwaymen rates. Wordie & Co. wanted the work, being already long

Opposite page: The inter-station horse parade at Buchanan Street goods station, Glasgow, on 1st July, 1950. This is a post-Wordie scene, but the number of horses still in service is impressive, though Scammell mechanical horses represent the new order. British Railways Board

established with the Great Northern, and following a valuation of the horses, vehicles and equipment at the LMS stables at Duncrue Street, by York Road Station, the contract was secured in early 1925. Wordie's bought the horses and vehicles and rented the stables, a move which led to the eventual closure of their first Belfast stables on Lagan Bank Road. They found, however, that they now had too many horses for their work in Belfast, unless they could find more contracts. They did increase their cartage for shipping companies and showed particular interest in the other railway steamer service, that between Belfast and Fleetwood, now also under the LMS, for whom Cowan & Co. had been carting since 1889. For their part Cowan & Co. wanted the Heysham work, and much argument followed, the main Wordie objection being that Cowan's were not agents for the LMS in Britain; it was also argued that they did not have enough horses in Belfast to do the work — they might even have to hire from Wordie's.

In the end the situation was resolved by the LMS, who in 1928 put three new ships, the "Dukes", on the Heysham run and closed the Fleetwood service as part of the rationalization of their shipping services. For a while the "Dukes" and the Fleetwood ships worked together, stretching Belfast cartage to the limit because of the size of the new ships. The LMS idea was for Cowan to have 60 per cent of the business and Wordie 40 per cent, but it did not work out like this, as Wordie's Belfast manager Mr Munro said in a letter to Glasgow on Monday, 30th April, 1928:

> From Saturday afternoon and all day Sunday [that morning the new *Duke of Lancaster* and the Fleetwood steamer arrived] we loaded up to 79 loads of goods for the town and sent 12 loads to the two railways on Saturday afternoon, and so far as we can gather Cowan did not load up more than 45 loads for the two days. They ran out of lorries on Saturday evening at 6 o'clock and yesterday [Sunday] at 1 o'clock were in the same position, and the whole onus was thrown on us to keep the work going, which we did.
>
> We were also out at 6 o'clock this morning and loaded up 10 loads before Cowan put in their appearance, as they had no horses or machines to cope with the work. You can quite understand that all their plant was loaded up on the Saturday afternoon and Sunday, or at least all they placed at the disposal of the shipping company. . .
>
> P.S. Monday, 30 April, Wordie dealt with 140 loads exclusive of railway traffic, Cowan & Co. 80.

The agreement reproduced above and on the opposite page was signed in 1926. It allowed Wordie & Co. to undertake cartage for the London, Midland & Scottish Railway (Northern Counties Committee) outside Belfast. Strathclyde Regional Archives

Munro adds that 75 to 100 loads were on the Belfast streets that Monday morning, and horses had to be brought in from Newry and Portaferry as well as extra parcel van horses, some of which were "very far through". The Saturday traffic must have been that which accumulated from the previous sailing as well as goods intended for the Sunday ships.

Please do not date
but return to be stamped

Memorandum of Agreement

Made the twenty seventh day of September One thousand nine hundred and twenty six Between The London Midland and Scottish Railway Company (Northern Counties Committee) having their principal Office at York Road in the City of Belfast (hereinafter called the Company which expression shall include their assigns when the context so requires or admits) of the one part and Archibald Watson and William Wordie of Number 75 west Nile Street Glasgow trading as Wordie & Company, Railway Agents and Carriers in Ireland and elsewhere (hereinafter called the Contractors) of the other part Whereas by Agreement dated the Twenty eighth day of August One thousand nine hundred and twenty five and made between the Company of the one part and the Contractors of the other part the Contractors undertook to perform certain services in connection with the collection Cartage and forwarding of goods booked by the Companys Railway And Whereas it has been agreed between the Company and the Contractors to extend the operation of the said Agreement to the several towns or places mentioned in the First Schedule hereto and that the said Agreement of the Twenty eighth day of August One thousand nine hundred and twenty five shall be applicable with regard to said towns and places as if the same had been expressly therein mentioned Save in so far as the same is hereby modified Now it is hereby agreed as follows:—

1.— This Agreement shall begin and take effect as from the First day of August One thousand nine hundred and twenty six and shall be determinable at the same time and in the same manner in all respects as the said Agreement of the Twenty eighth day of August One thousand nine hundred and twenty five. Notice of intention to terminate this Agreement may be served by either party to affect any one or more of the Stations or places mentioned in the First Schedule hereto and such notice shall not affect any Station or place not therein expressly mentioned.

2.— The Contractors shall not be required to maintain Offices or Stores in the towns or places mentioned in the First Schedule hereto and all communications for the Contractors relating to the collection delivery and booking of Goods and parcels at any such Station may be addressed to them in care of the Companys Station Master at such Station and Clause 7 of the said Agreement with the necessary modifications shall apply to such business.—

3.— The Contractors shall carry out at each of the Stations and places in the said First Schedule the duties specified as regards Belfast in Clauses 7. 8. and 9 of said Agreement and also (save at Stations where the delivery of parcels is made by the Companys servants) the duties specified in

With the Heysham steamer contract won, Wordie & Co. sought work outside Belfast at the stations of the LMS, Londonderry and elsewhere, where the railway were still carting for themselves. As Wordie's hoped, the railway gave it up and the company in 1926 secured the work at Antrim, Ballymena, Ballymoney, Coleraine, Limavady, Portrush and Whitehead; Londonderry followed in 1929. Apart from the Londonderry stables these were all small depots, five or six horses at Ballymena and only one at Limavady, while at Portrush, where the LMS hotel stables were used, the horses were out to grass in the summer. There were also three small depots between Ballymena and Ballymoney, Cullibackey, Glarryford and Killagan, but they did not stay in use for long.

Although expansion was the order of the day in Northern Ireland the company was facing economic problems, as were the railways they served. The industrial climate was unstable, with the post-war boom followed by a post-war slump; labour unrest culminated in the General Strike of 1926. In addition the railways were facing their first challenge ever, from competitive road transport. The late twenties were not good years for Wordie & Co.; they were losing money. In 1925 the firm lost £384, and in 1929 the loss was £2,992. These figures included the work for the former Great North of Scotland Railway outside Aberdeen, which was always profitable; without it the losses in 1929 would have been £6,154. Cuts had to be made; horses were disposed of and fewer were bought, men were laid off.

Yet with their newly acquired powers to operate road services throughout, the railways were expanding their road haulage interests. In 1931 the LMS began making overtures to the partners of Wordie & Co. and in August, 1932, agreement was reached that the LMS should have a 51 per cent stake in Wordie & Co.; from 1933 the firm was called Wordie & Co. Ltd, with a Board of Directors. Archibald Watson and William Wordie as Managing Directors were joined by two directors from the LMS, John Ballantyne, the Chief Goods Manager, who had been Goods Manager at Glasgow, and Ernest Lemon, Vice-President of the LMS, with responsibility over the operations and commercial divisions of the company; he was followed by W. Yeaman.

Work for the former Great North of Scotland Railway outside Aberdeen was left out of this since the contract was with the rival London & North Eastern, and eventually a new company, Wordie's (North Eastern) Ltd., was created to handle it; this company remained under family control. Left out, too, was the Irish business. Here the LMS had been keen for Wordie's to take over all railway cartage in Ulster jointly with themselves and the Great Northern. These proposals had been put forward in 1931, the

LMS being concerned at the enterprise of the Great Northern, with their Railhead Scheme of motor lorry services from railway stations running to a timetable in connection with the trains.

After discussions over the formation of what might have been called Wordie & Co. (Ireland) Ltd, half of which was to be under the Wordie partnership and half to be shared between the LMS and Great Northern, nothing happened because the Wordie partnership thought the railways would dominate them in Northern Ireland. Eventually the Irish business was resolved by the creation of new family companies, Wordie & Co., Dublin, and in 1937 Wordie & Co. (Ulster) Ltd. Wordie & Co., Dublin, was a convenience to keep the business in the Free State as an entity, while Wordie (Ulster) was an independent creation to fight the Northern Ireland Road Transport Board, established in 1935, whose damaging policy is described below. Also outside LMS control was the old Glasgow cartage firm of R. Grierson, from 1935 re-formed as R. Grierson & Co. Ltd but wholly under Wordie family control and wearing the Wordie colours.

While the family were pursuing these independent lines, the bulk of the Wordie organization remained under strong railway influence. Under the LMS, with their large capital reserves, a policy of expansion was possible and was pursued to serve the best interests of the railway company. By the mid nineteen-thirties the road haulage industry was operating on firmer foundations as a result of commissions of inquiry and legislation. The unbridled cut-throat competition of the nineteen-twenties was recognized by the Government and reported on by a Royal Commission which started work in November, 1928, issuing its findings in three volumes, the last of which appeared in December, 1930.

Meanwhile a Road Traffic Act had become law on 1st August, 1930. This attempted to regulate the use of the roads by limiting hours of work and enforcing rest periods for commercial drivers. It also demanded driving licences, fixed the minimum age for a driver and asked for a declaration of physical fitness. Third-party insurance was compulsory, speed limits were imposed and licences could be endorsed or suspended. On motor lorries second men were needed if trailers were in use, because of their cable-worked mechanical brakes operated from the left-hand side of the cab. The Act was a start in the right direction, but there were defects. There was no driving test; that came in 1935, and the system of grouping vehicles for tests and licences followed in 1937. Nor was there any test for physical fitness (there still is not), while it was impossible to enforce the hours of work limits and rest periods.

The defects were soon seen and a further Act was passed in 1933 to plug the gaps, following the Transport Conference chaired by Sir Arthur Salter which reported in August, 1932. This was a

Below: *At the rear of the motor lorry the sheet was folded like the end of a parcel and roped across twice with diagonal ropes as additional security.*

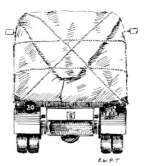

Robert Fulton with his working companion in the Divis Street yard, Belfast. Robert Fulton

confrontation of rail and road interests to try to find a balanced transport policy for the country. A principal recommendation was that road users should pay more towards road upkeep and improvement: a perennial cry, recognized as early as 1909, when Lloyd George set up the Road Fund. The Development and Road Improvement Funds Act of that year introduced both a tax on motor vehicles and on petrol, the idea being that the revenue would pay for road works. Unfortunately the revenue proved too lucrative for successive governments to resist and more and more funds were diverted to the Exchequer. Eventually in 1936 road funding methods were altered, estimates were presented and the roads received whatever money Parliament saw fit to grant them.

The Road and Rail Traffic Act of 1933 was an improvement on its predecessor. Driving hours and rest periods were amended for drivers of commercial vehicles, and from 1st October, 1934, they had to keep log books in which their hours and journeys were recorded. These were liable to sudden inspection, so they had to be kept up to date. Herbert Knox comments on how strictly Wordie's observed the law. They ordered the new restrictions on drivers to be observed for a week before the Act came into force, to iron out difficulties. Probably they were the only haulage firm in the country to do this; others ignored the new Act, or at least tried to do so, even when it became law.

More thought was now given to the licensing and taxation of motor vehicles on commercial work. Annual licences were dependent on the condition of the vehicle and on the log book records, and there were three grades of licence: A was to carry goods for hire and reward anywhere; B was for hire and reward in a defined area and to carry in connection with the owner's own business, for example a coal merchant; C was granted for carriage on behalf of the owner's own business only.

At the same time the trades unions were securing better rewards for their members. There had been a mass of small organizations growing out of the old friendly societies, but more influential bodies were emerging, notably the Scottish Horse and Motormen's Association, whose early years have been described briefly in Chapter four. By the nineteen-thirties they had large funds, but, as their historian Angela Tuckett says, no very forceful leadership.

Quite otherwise was the command exercised by Ernest Bevin over his enormous Transport & General Workers' Union, which he built to a size which could not be ignored. Pressure from him led to the passage of the Road Haulage Wages Act of 1938 and the establishment of wage-negotiating machinery on a national level.

Opposite the unions were the employers' associations. The Glasgow Horse and Motorman's Association (not to be confused with the trade union) was formed in 1933, amalgamating with the Scottish Carriers' and Haulage Contractors' Association and the Central Scotland Hauliers' Association. In 1945 this amalgamated body became the Scottish branch of the Road Haulage Association. There was also a Scottish Railway Road Carriers' Association whose members, although commercial rivals, met to discuss mutual problems; members included Wordie's, Cowan's, Mutter Howey's, Cameron's and the smaller people.

Nobody remembers quite what was being celebrated, but this horse at Fraserburgh is clearly decorated for some special occasion; he might have been about to take part in one of the parades organized by such bodies as the Scottish Horse and Motormen's Association.
George A. Dey

In Ireland the same unbridled competition on the roads had led to similar controlling legislation both in the Free State and in Northern Ireland. That in Northern Ireland was passed in 1926, four years before Westminster's Road Traffic Act, for which the Stormont legislation served as a model. At the same time both the Dublin and the Stormont governments recognized the danger to the railways of road transport; Acts of 1927 passed by both allowed the railways to run their own road services, both passenger and goods. Both the Great Northern and the LMS took full

Below: *Among the sights of Glasgow was the carriage of complete locomotives from the North British Locomotive Works in Springburn down to the big crane on Stobcross Quay. Road Engines & Kerr, who joined Wordie's in 1937, handled the work by steam and motor haulage. The silhouette shows the* Burrell Simplicity *heading the* Fowler Supreme *with a 4-6-0 for the Egyptian State Railways in 1947.*

advantage of these measures, the Great Northern with their Railhead Scheme being helped by further Free State legislation in 1932 which repealed the 1927 Act, giving the railways in Eire extra powers to acquire road undertakings. This new legislation from Dublin not only made licensing compulsory but made sure that road and rail competition was either restricted or banned.

In Northern Ireland, however, competition persisted, with ever more harmful effects on the railways. A committee of inquiry was called, chaired by Sir Felix Pole of the Great Western Railway; the committee recommended more co-ordination of rail and road transport, for they had found not so much that the railways were losing traffic to the roads but that while the roads were able to attract new traffic the railways failed to do so. Sir Felix's ideas for co-ordination were incorporated in the Road and Rail Traffic Act (Northern Ireland) of 1935, which interpreted them as proposals for nationalization. It created the Northern Ireland Road Transport Board to acquire all bus and lorry undertakings in the province with the exception of Belfast Municipal Transport. Far from helping the railways, the new Board did much damage by running services in opposition. At the same time it suffered by being a common carrier, having to take all that was offered. For Wordie & Co. the Board was an obstacle: it took over all long-distance work, leaving Wordie's with local collection and delivery, much of it dependent on Great Northern and LMS contracts; because of the heightened road competition these companies had less business to pass on. Wordie's answer was the creation of an independent company in Northern Ireland, Wordie & Co. (Ulster) Ltd, to build up work for themselves.

With their new road powers the LMS in mainland Britain wasted no time in developing haulage interests. To Wordie & Co. Ltd were now added satellites, all of them with motors, none with horses. By 1938 the Inverness hauliers J. C. Brooke & Co. Ltd had been bought, with eight motors and two trailers. R. J. Ironside recalls that Brooke's were well established, with an A licence

136

operating to Wick and Glasgow, carrying general merchandise, livestock, steel and timber, and with special trailers for electrical cable drums.

An A licence was difficult to acquire, the usual solution being to buy a business which already had one. The acquisition of J. C. Brooke with their expertise and their contracts gave Wordie's a new dimension in Inverness. Another purchase was Herbert Davidson Ltd, of Edinburgh, with sixteen motors. Also into the fold came John Russell & Son, of West Calder, near Bathgate, about half way between Glasgow and Edinburgh, with seventeen motors, and a host of operators from south-west Scotland, where Wordie & Co. had never penetrated except for Stranraer, since they had never won a contract with the Glasgow & South Western Railway. But this was now LMS territory.

From Dumfries came James Dickson, with eleven lorries and three motor coaches, and Dumfries & Galloway Transport, with ten motors; from Lockerbie South Western Transports, with eighteen motors; from Kirkcudbright Duke Gordon's fleet of eight or so Fords, which Wordie's replaced by Albions; from Stranraer Kelly's Haulage; and from Glasgow James Walker, with five motors.

Also from Glasgow came Road Engines & Kerr, who specialized in heavy haulage, particularly of locomotives from the North British Locomotive Company's works to the docks for export. Their history has been well covered by Tom McTaggart in his book *Pioneers of Heavy Haulage*, published by Alloway Publishing of Ayr in 1985. They were an amalgamation in 1932 of two firms, William Kerr & Co., who started operations with one steam traction engine in 1899, and the Road Steam Engine Co. Ltd, who were founded in 1870. Mr McTaggart has given vivid descriptions of their work. The Road Steam Engine Co. Ltd used Thomson vertical-boilered road steamers, while Kerr's employed Burrells, McLarens, Fowlers and Foden steam lorries. Both companies fared badly during the depression, hence the amalgamation, but they still lacked capital to re-equip. In 1936 negotiations were opened with Wordie & Co.

E. W. PAGET-TOMLINSON

William Watson, who joined the Wordie Board in 1934 on the death of his elder brother Archie. He is seen wearing RNVR uniform.

Robert Dougall Fyfe joined Wordie & Co. in 1889 at Stirling and in 1910 became general manager, a post he retained until 1947. This picture was taken at Newcastle before 1910.
James P. Fyfe

Ltd, and the transfer was effected the following year. The name Road Engines & Kerr was kept and the fleet of traction engines and trailers was augmented by new Scammell low loaders and ERF articulated lorries. Like Wordie & Co. Ltd, Road Engines & Kerr passed into nationalization in 1948. By 1938 Wordie's, within the LMS organization, had 253 motor lorries and 824 horses, and independently 19 motors and 260 horses.

Finally there was the 1937 merger with Currie & Co. in Newcastle, with the reciprocal agreement that Currie's would close their Glasgow office. Currie's also took over Wordie's depot in Leeds, which had been established in 1933. Herbert Knox has written about this in some detail, for it was he who set it up. Securing return loads from the West Riding was one reason for the depot's creation, but Wordie's were anxious to build up new business in the area, for they had just lost their major Newcastle customer, Northern Clubs Federation Brewery. The depots at Newcastle and Leeds had done well, building up a large warehousing and trunk road haulage organization which made up for their loss of railway work when the London & North Eastern was created in 1923.

On the family side there had been changes. Archie Watson died suddenly in 1934. He was cruising off Lochinver in Sutherland when he suffered acute appendicitis; although the yacht headed for the mainland and he was rushed to Glasgow by car and train he died before surgery could be undertaken. His place on the Board was taken by his younger brother William, who was by profession an electrical engineer but by inclination a mariner. He had served in the Dover Patrol in the First World War and won the DSO at Zeebrugge as commander of a smoke-screen layer; he enjoyed the rank of a full commander, RNVR. William Wordie stayed as Managing Director and the two LMS men continued on the Board of Wordie & Co. Ltd. The family companies, Wordie's North-Eastern, Wordie (Ulster) and Wordie, Dublin, and also Grierson's, had their own Boards, while the general manager of both the family businesses and of the railway-controlled business was Robert Dougall Fyfe, who had joined Wordie's in 1889 and became General Manager in 1910.

During the Second World War Wordie & Co. Ltd became a controlled undertaking under the Ministry of War Transport, with other companies attached to it to receive their orders; an example was J. D. Smith of Inverness, who ran a fleet of Dennises under an A licence, with their depot by the harbour at Clachnaharry, where the Caledonian Canal enters the Beauly Firth. The war involved Wordie & Co. in much extra work. The building of an airfield at Wick, started in 1939, necessitated the transport of materials which came by rail, and a steam crane was kept busy in the goods yard transferring them from rail to road. One of the Wordie Albion five-tonners was on this job, and another Wordie Albion was sent to the Shetlands to help in defence works, based at Lerwick. R. J. Ironside, who remembers all this, was the mechanic who serviced this scattered fleet. He also recalls carrying timber to shore up damaged bulkheads in a capital ship which had been torpedoed in the Atlantic but had managed to reach the Minch and anchor in Loch Torridon in November, 1939; Wordie five-ton Albion No 154 was commandeered along with others to fetch the timber from sawmills at Inverness. The journey was not without incident because No 154 struck a soft patch of road west of Achnasheen and sank in. A recovery vehicle was sent, and Rod Ironside followed in the District Manager's Morris Eight, which doubled as a service utility. It took four days to dig the lorry out and lay a roadbed of sleepers, but all was completed by late Saturday afternoon. Then the engine would not start, due to a damp and short-circuited magneto. After two hours' baking in the oven of the Achnasheen Hotel the magneto was refitted, and all was ready. But the Torridon policeman who had kept a watch on the whole operation was not impressed when told of the plan to start early the following morning: "Ye canna work on the Sabbath," he said, and rode away on his cycle. In the morning No 154 quietly moved off to Torridon pier.

Further south Wordie & Co. were engaged in the transport of munitions unloaded from ships in the Clyde to assembly sites and depots in and around Glasgow. Crated-up military vehicles were a major part of the work, in which Cowan & Co. shared. The Divis Street stables in Belfast were set ablaze by incendiary bombs during an air raid in 1941. With great presence of mind the horsekeepers released the horses as fire took hold. Panic stricken, the horses galloped in a body to Jordanstown on the shores of Belfast Lough, but all were later rounded up safe as they grazed in the fields, as Robert Fulton and Joe Galway remember. They were not the only Wordie stables to suffer: during the Glasgow blitz the stables in West Street, Tradeston, were also destroyed by fire, and Mrs McInnes of Penilee, Glasgow, recalls the panic-stricken horses that had to be released. She says the Royal Navy were sent in to rescue people and calm the horses, some of them with their tails on fire and mad with fear. Two men in particular she remembers doing sterling work to save the horses; one of them was given an award for his bravery.

A sidelight on Wordie's war operations was the sending of lorries to Europe in the wake of the Allied armies to help rebuild the shattered transport system on the Continent. One at least was sent from the Inverness depot, as James Hendry remembers, for work in France, Holland and Germany; it bore the title "European

Relief" on the cab headboard. The sight of others reminded war-weary Scottish soldiers of peace, not without a touch of homesickness.

After the war Wordie & Co. Ltd revived their fleet by the acquisition of vehicles which had been on war service, Inverness receiving seventeen ERFs which had been on munitions work, it is thought in France. They were now busy on post-war reconstruction and development, including the Glen Affric hydro-electric scheme, for which James Hendry drove an ERF seven tonner, fleet No 535, from Beauly station to Cannich and Mullardoch, carrying equipment. He made two daily runs to Cannich and one to Mullardoch, where a tunnel was being built, a total of 140 miles at around 20 mph. Another post-war job was the transport of aero engines from Dalcross airfield to the nearest station, Gollanfield, the junction for Fort George on the Inverness–Nairn line, from where they went by rail to England. Commers were used on this work.

But the end was near for large-scale road haulage in private hands. The 1945 Labour Government had elaborate plans for nationalization of transport and much else. Some form of public control had already been considered for the railways, which had been under Government direction throughout the war, under a Railway Executive Committee as in 1914–18, although railway management itself looked forward to a return to private administration, with more integration between the groups.

The case for nationalizing road haulage was not so strong, although the aim to create an integrated transport system in which rail, road and water could each play a useful part was laudable enough and entirely in line with Labour thinking. Road haulage organization was, however, most complex and difficult to assemble under one authority, bearing in mind the A, B and C types of licence, the C licence vehicles being operated by every variety of

E. W. PAGET-TOMLINSON

private firm, who could hardly be expected to surrender their road fleets. Originally, indeed, it had been proposed to nationalize A, B and C fleets, but so many amendments were admitted as the Bill passed through Parliament that the 1947 Transport Act turned out differently from what had been intended. The new British Transport Commission acquired only a part of the long-distance (that is, over 25 miles) road transport industry because C licence haulage was left out, as were some specialized hauliers, those engaged in furniture removals, bulk liquid, meat and livestock transport, plus certain other exceptional work.

The Act, which came into force on 1st January, 1948, established the British Transport Commission to supervise several executives each responsible for an aspect of inland transport: the Railway Executive, the Docks and Inland Waterways Executive, and for road transport the Road Haulage Executive. Familiarly the nationalized road fleet was called British Road Services, or BRS, and was divided into regional divisions, of which there were eight; these were in turn divided into districts, themselves divided into groups, of which there were 204 in 1952, at about the peak of BRS numerical strength. The title of the group was painted on the side of the vehicle; thus Perth Group, Oldham Group.

Absorption into the nationalized authority was compulsory for long-distance hauliers and for those associated with the now nationalized railways. Wordie & Co. Ltd and its subsidiaries fell into both categories, as did the Wordie companies in mainland Britain which were independent of the LMS, that is Wordie's (North Eastern), who had bought their last horses in 1945, and Grierson's. Wordie's (North Eastern) was sold in 1946; Grierson's ceased trading at the end of 1947, their horses and vehicles being sold to the British Transport Commission, although Grierson's carried on for a while as an investment company.

The transfer of Wordie & Co. Ltd and its subsidiaries to state control was not direct, for the Wordie family disposed of their interest to the LMS some months before nationalization; the railway company, therefore, were the sole owners on 1st January, 1948. Under full LMS control the Wordie name was retained, as it was for a year or so under nationalization as Wordie & Co. B.T.C. Ltd; thereafter it became simply British Road Services under the various group headings in Scotland and North-east England. In Ireland the Wordie name lived on, although the Dublin business had been sold in 1946/47; Wordie (Ulster) escaped the mainland nationalization and stayed in business for over two decades.

Mr Tom Atkin had the task of taking over Wordie interests in South-west Scotland on behalf of British Road Services. These included their depots at Dumfries, Kirkcudbright, Stranraer, where there were still four horses, Abington and Braehead near

Carstairs. He had, and retains, a high opinion of the company, well run with well-maintained vehicles. They tended, he says, to keep to themselves and not to work in with other hauliers, being conscious of their long service to the railways. They did not for this reason develop long-distance work as much as they could have done, certainly not much outside Scotland; allied to their higher-than-others rates was their concentration on local work, a roll of chicken wire here, a couple of sacks of sugar there, all making them less profitable than they could have been.

The *Stirling Observer* published an obituary of Wordie & Co. on 26th September, 1950, on the occasion of the removal of the Wordie name from their Thistle Street office in Stirling, the town where it all began. It was headed "After Two Centuries, Old Stirling Name Disappears, Victim of Nationalization", and it gave a brief account of the company's beginnings. The Wordie name was replaced by British Road Services Douglas Group, another fine old Scots name, commented the writer, but in this case it referred to the Douglas telephone area of Glasgow.

To end the Wordie saga in Scotland here are a couple of anecdotes from Mr Archibald McGill, once a policeman in Falkirk, giving the police viewpoint on road transport:

In 1933/34 I was a policeman in Falkirk and Wordie and Company had a yard at the rear of Wordie's Buildings in Graham's Road, Falkirk, where their stables were. I was a single man, stationed in Denny, but I was married on 4th April, 1933, transferring to Falkirk on 19th May, 1933, when my Chief Constable allocated me a house. I think I would be about a month in my house in Falkirk, when, on my day off, possibly on the first week in June, 1933, my wife suggested that we might go up town, as it was such a lovely day.

So we set off and went up town, and when walking along Newmarket Street my wife remarked on the crowd of people flocking down that street on the right. "Where are they all going to?" The street on the right just happened to be Hope Street, which leads down to Brockville Park, the home ground of Falkirk F.C. When I told her this she said, "But there's no football on today, is there?" I told her that there would probably be a greyhound meeting on.

She then expressed a desire to see a greyhound race, and we made for Brockville Park. I warned her that she had better put cotton wool in her ears, as the language would not be very choice. The first race she saw was enough for her, and she suggested going out to the Dollar Park. Thus we headed up Hope Street towards Camelon Road, en route for the Dollar Park, when I heard her giggling to herself, and I asked her, "What's the joke?"

"The joke is that you are always saying that observation is the Pc's greatest attribute, yet you seem to be walking about with your eyes closed." She pointed to a Wordie's horse-drawn lorry, moving north in Hope Street towards Brockville Park, or Meeks Road. The driver of the horse-drawn vehicle was sitting on the front left-hand side of the lorry with his legs dangling outside the left shaft of the lorry. His right hand was under his sack-cloth apron, and my wife, pointing to the gutter at the edge of the pavement in front of us, then said, "Now look back at the lorry and see where the water is coming from." I did so, and the "water" was coming from immediately under the driver sitting on his lorry. "Now, what do you call that offence?"

I replied, "Committing a nuisance, but then there are extenuating circumstances." "Such as?" she asked. I replied, "He is in charge of a horse-drawn vehicle, and cannot leave it unattended." We carried on to the Dollar Park, and spent a nice day in the sun.

The second anecdote was one of the most puzzling I have ever come across. I was on night duty on Grahamston beat, which extends from Grahamston railway bridge the full length of Graham's Road, right to Grahamston–Bainsford canal bridge. About one in the morning, as I was making towards Falkirk Foundry Security Office, where we were in the habit of taking our night-shift break for a meal, I was overtaken by a Wordie's motor lorry, which headed north to Bainsford over the canal bridge. An hour later, as I was leaving to resume my beat in Graham's Road, I saw the same Wordie's lorry and, keeping it in sight, I saw it carry on over the canal bridge into Bainsford. About three that morning I had occasion to examine property in Cowan Avenue, a street leading off Graham's Road towards the west, and on returning to Graham's Road, I examined the security

One of the Dundee Albions in British Road Services colours but still displaying its Wordie fleet number 651. It is an FT3 with a six-cylinder petrol engine. This vehicle was delivered new to Wordie's in 1946, with William Binnie as driver. He is the driver in this 1948 carnival scene.
William Binnie

of the property on the west side of Graham's Road, as far as Western Avenue. This same lorry now came down Graham's Road towards me and headed north, eventually passing over the canal bridge into Bainsford. About 4 am the same thing happened, the same lorry crossed the canal bridge into Bainsford.

About 4.45 am I entered the railway goods yard at Springfield to have a word with the railway constable who was in charge there, and I was about to return to Graham's Road when the same lorry passed north again. At no time had I been in a position to stop the lorry, as it always seemed to be passing as I was returning to Graham's Road. Still puzzling over the matter, I made my way to Hope Street Police Office to reach there about 5.50 am to sign off duty. As I entered the office, I heard the phone ring and Sgt George Stephen went to answer it. He returned to the general office almost immediately and told me to take the office bike and proceed to Bainsford Cross, where a motor lorry had collided with a tramcar; the roadway was blocked with a load of orange boxes which had fallen from the lorry. He told me that the driver of the tramcar was Leslie Smith and the motor lorry was a Wordie's one. He suggested that I call at Wordie's Buildings in Graham's Road and call out John McNee, the foreman, to clear the roadway.

John McNee was known to most of the police, and I summoned him to attend to the clearance of the load.

On my arrival at Bainsford Cross I saw the tram driver, and he suggested to me that the driver of the Wordie motor lorry might be the worse for drink. I saw that the lorry that had collided with the tram was the same one that I had seen so often during the night. For an instant I smiled to myself as I thought the driver would be more likely to be dizzy than drunk, after going round in circles all night.

I asked the tram driver where the lorry driver was, and he said he was round the back end of the lorry. After a minute or two I realised that the driver was playing hide and seek with me. However, I came face to face with him, and I asked him if he was the driver of the lorry.

He admitted that he was, and I asked him where he was going. He told me that he had been sent to Leith Docks with the lorry, and he did not know the road, so he had stopped when he saw a policeman at Dennyloanhead, and the latter had told him to carry straight on until he came to the tramcar rails at Camelon, and to follow the tramcar rails all the way, and this he had done.

I know I took the driver to the Police Station, as he smelt of drink, but I cannot recollect if the doctor certified him incapable or not. He certainly was not driving as though he was under the influence during the night, but he had collided with the first tramcar he had met in the morning. The collision had happened at the Bainsford loop, where a single line from Carron Road became a double line at Bainsford Cross. Anyway, John McNee asked me if my wife had a pram, and when I said we had, he told me to send her round to the stables that afternoon with the pram. I did so, and we were eating Jaffa oranges for weeks afterwards.

This would probably have taken place about June or July, 1934.

144

Wordie & Co. (Ulster) Ltd   10

FOLLOWING the decision to operate independently in Northern Ireland, on 4th August, 1937, the directors of the new company, Wordie & Co. (Ulster) Ltd, met in Glasgow. They were Colonel William Wordie and Mr Robert D. Fyfe, with Mr Victor Treble as secretary; Mr Treble was also secretary of the main company.

Colonel Wordie was appointed chairman and it was agreed to buy the Northern Ireland business of Wordie & Co. Ltd from that company, subject to a licence to operate being granted under the 1935 Road and Rail Traffic Act. The price was £11,000. Mention was made at the meeting of five vehicles transferred to the Northern Ireland Road Transport Board earlier in the year. These represented about a third of the small fleet of motors that Wordie's had in Ulster at that time, Leylands, Albions, and Morris parcels vans, so the new company was left mainly with horses in Belfast and the outstations, although the 12th November, 1938, number of *Modern Transport* did list ten motors and three trailers in the Wordie (Ulster) fleet. Their first motor in Northern Ireland had been a half-ton Ford van bought from the LMS in 1924.

So Wordie & Co. (Ulster) Ltd went to work in the province undertaking storage and cartage contracts for firms such as Player's and Tate & Lyle, the local delivery work for the Great Northern and the LMS, and for the Heysham and Glasgow steamers. The railway and steamer work involved not only deliveries to customers but cartage between stations and between stations and quays. Belfast was the main centre for this, but there was similar work at Londonderry and at the outstations.

In Derry there was a local cartage contract with the Londonderry & Lough Swilly Railway, a three-foot-gauge line to Letterkenny and into Donegal, eventually reaching the Atlantic at Burtonport. The railway company also ran buses and lorries. Like the Great Northern, the Lough Swilly operated in both Northern Ireland and the Free State, customs examinations hampering operation; the Great Northern crossed the frontier no fewer than ten times.

Wordie (Ulster) started with modest profits and dividends (for example, a three per cent dividend in 1939), but the Second World War soon brought increased business; in 1940 a 10 per cent dividend was declared. William Watson joined the Ulster board in

A Ransomes & Rapier mobile crane loads a Wordie (Ulster) Leyland in a Belfast goods yard during the Second World War. The white mudguards and blackout headlamp low down at the front give clues to the date. The drawing is taken from a photograph in the Ryan Collection in Belfast Public Libraries. Drawn by kind permission of Belfast Public Libraries.

1941, and the company stayed rewardingly stable until the end of the war. Being in Ulster it remained free from nationalization in 1948 when Wordie & Co. Ltd themselves, by then wholly owned by the London, Midland & Scottish Railway, passed into British Road Services. The last meeting in the Wordie offices at 46 West George Street, Glasgow, was held on 5th March, 1948; henceforward for some years the business was to be directed by Mr Fyfe from a room in the offices of Thomson, Jackson, Gourlay and Taylor, chartered accountants, at 24 George Square, Glasgow. Mr David Taylor became company secretary in March, 1948, in succession to Mr Treble; this same month saw James Mann Wordie elected to the board.

Meanwhile the transport scene in Northern Ireland was in a state of flux. The Great Northern Railway remained for a while independent, although increasingly precarious financially. By 1950 there was danger of immediate closure, but the railway was saved by a new administration, the Great Northern Railway Board, backed by the Eire and the Northern Ireland governments. The

new arrangement took effect on 1st September, 1953, but it was only a stopgap, for on 1st October, 1958, the Great Northern was split between the transport undertakings of each country, Coras Iompair Eireann in the South, the Ulster Transport Authority in the North. This Ulster Transport Authority was a creation of the Stormont Parliament to acquire rail and road transport undertakings wholly within Northern Ireland. It came into being on 1st October, 1948, but the undertakings took some time to acquire. The London, Midland & Scottish (Northern Counties Committee) actually became, because of the LMS link, a part of the British Railway Executive for a while, until bought on 1st April, 1949, from the British Transport Commission by the Ulster Transport Authority. By this time the Belfast & County Down Railway was already in UTA hands; indeed it was taken over immediately, in the autumn of 1948, as was the Northern Ireland Road Transport Board, both buses and lorries, acquired by the UTA on 1st October, 1948. The Bill for the UTA had spoken of powers to take over any road haulage concern in Ulster, and this was discussed at a board meeting of Wordie (Ulster) in May, 1948. An alternative possibility was for a company like Wordie's to offer to be taken over.

In 1948 Wordie (Ulster) committed themselves more positively to motor transport. Hitherto they had run a few lorries and vans, but now a Karrier Bantam tractor and trailer were delivered to Belfast and tried out to see how they compared with the horses. They must have been satisfactory, because in 1949 twelve motors were brought over, and four more trailers. It was reported that one Karrier did the work of two and half horses. In 1949, too, the Ulster Transport Authority approached Wordie (Ulster) with a view to purchase, but nothing came of this. There were now much improved trading results, and a 25 per cent dividend was paid in 1950, but the future did not look so good, with the threatened break-up of the Great Northern. Wage increases were constantly being demanded, not without some justification, but to cover them rates had to rise. Another problem in 1951 was higher hay charges; hay was bought locally, but some of the oats was shipped over from Scotland.

To stay profitable there had to be retrenchment, and 1952 saw the start of closures of outstations of the former Northern Counties Committee, along with closure of the Duncrue Street stables in Belfast. On 31st December, 1951, contracts at the remaining NCC outstations expired; these were Antrim, Ballymena, Ballymoney, Coleraine, Larne, Limavady, Londonderry and Portrush. On closure horses and equipment were transferred to Belfast for disposal, the horses often being sold at well over their stock value, even double. The Great Northern outstations were to go in 1955;

Divis Street yard in the nineteen-fifties, when Wordie (Ulster) had the contract with the Glasgow–Belfast steamers. Note the nosebag on the lorry and the skids slung underneath, also the wheels with steel hubs which made them freer running. Alan Campbell

these were Armagh, Dungannon, Enniskillen, Newry, Omagh and Strabane. The exception was Londonderry, where Great Northern railway work was kept until 1963, although by then no longer Great Northern. On 31st May, 1952, the NCC, or rather Ulster Transport Authority, contract in Belfast itself expired; it was not renewed. The only railway work left was with the Great Northern in Londonderry and Belfast, but there were still contracts with the Heysham steamers of the British Transport Commission and with the Burns & Laird steamers to Glasgow. In Londonderry the contract was for delivery from the Heysham and Glasgow steamers to the railways; the Heysham–Londonderry service, like the Glasgow–Londonderry, was in the hands of Burns & Laird. Additionally Wordie's had private customers for whom goods were stored and carried, but only local three-and-half-mile-radius cartage was undertaken, since the UTA continued to do the outside work inherited from the Road Transport Board.

Although cartage work suffered restriction, new vehicles were needed to maintain an efficient service, so more Karrier Bantam tractors and trailers, a rigid Bantam and a three-ton Albion were ordered in 1952; there was twelve months' delivery on the Karriers. There were still horses at Belfast and at Londonderry, although at Londonderry it was thought four two-ton motors could do all the work. In 1953 the Londonderry depot lost its business with the Lough Swilly Railway because the line closed.

By this time there were changes on the board. Colonel William Wordie died on 19th April, 1952, and was replaced as chairman by his brother James. Then on 13th January, 1954, William Watson died; John Wordie, James's eldest son, took his place on the board. Then on 8th December, 1958, Mr Robert D. Fyfe died. He had, said Sir James Wordie, been associated with Wordie & Co. for over sixty-nine years, surely a record for length of service to any business enterprise. Aged eighty-three at the time of his death, he had joined the company from school at the age of thirteen in 1889. He was born in Stirling, the son of an engine driver, and his first job was in Wordie & Co.'s Stirling office. He moved to Aberdeen, Edinburgh, Belfast, Newcastle-upon-Tyne and eventually Glasgow, where in 1910 he was made the company's general manager. Sir James Wordie paid a further tribute: "His knowledge and experience in the cartage business had been unequalled." He had remained in harness to the last.

In spite of the growth of motor transport, horses were still being bought in 1954, the last being a black and brown gelding acquired in June of that year; he was a six-year-old of seventeen hands. In 1955 there were thirty-nine horses in Belfast and eight in Londonderry, as against thirty-seven motors in Belfast and five in Derry. Although prone to lose money, horses were still the best on some traffic, for example on the Spillers flour deliveries in Derry from ship to store, a short run on level ground on which five lorries were employed.

Sir James Wordie, CBE, who became chairman on his brother's death in 1952.   P. J. Wordie

R. D. Fyfe, who had been associated with Wordie's for nearly seventy years when he died in 1958.
James P. Fyfe

Economies in horse management were made, shoeing being done by contractors, while at Derry feed was bought locally and made up in the stables instead of being sent over from the company's provender department in Belfast. Moves to buy prepared feed from outside for Belfast were discussed, but never acted upon. However, the saddlery shop there was closed in 1956; again outsiders could do the work more economically.

Warehousing, long established, as Chapter seven describes, became in the nineteen-fifties an increasing part of the company's business as the cartage contracts dwindled, stable accommodation in Belfast being converted into storage. To keep pace with the needs of their customers Wordie's had to install mechanical handling equipment: in 1951 six new hoists were authorized at Divis Street and later board meetings discussed elevators and conveyors of various patterns, along with lifting trucks and stillages, the frames on which goods are laid. Storage customers included Kelloggs, Gallagher's tobacco, ICI, Lever Brothers and British Oil and Cake Mills, who were also at Derry, the Ministry of Agriculture, who stored potato flour, and the washing powder makers Thomas Hedley, later Procter & Gamble. Much cartage was done for these firms. Occasionally there were problems like the three tons of flax which nobody claimed, the missing cases of salmon from a consignment stored by the Ministry of Food in the early nineteen-forties, and the stolen cartons of Player's cigarettes.

By the later nineteen-fifties the earlier motor vehicles were being withdrawn, including the parcels vans which had been in

service since the nineteen-thirties. But many new motors and trailers were being ordered: Bantams and Dyson trailers, three- and four-ton Commers. Two Bedfords, a 5/6 ton and a three-ton, were bought in early 1956 from the liquidators of a Londonderry haulage company, J. R. Montgomery, who had had the cartage contract with the County Donegal Railways. By the purchase Wordie's secured Montgomery's contract with Burns & Laird, which gave them the delivery work from the Heysham and Glasgow steamers to the city; hitherto Wordie's had had only the railway cartage from these ships. Montgomery's twenty horses were sold.

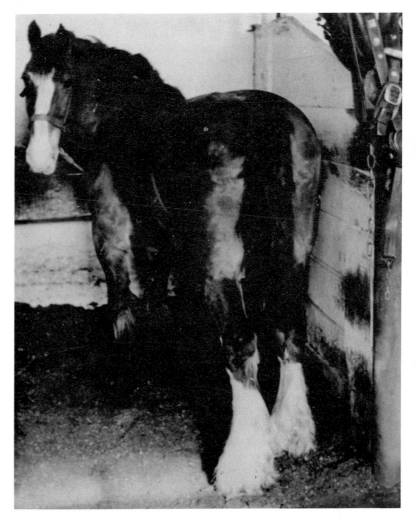

Horses served the Wordies well for nearly a hundred and twenty years up to 1961, when brutal economics brought their reign to an end. This horse is in the Divis Street stables in Belfast.
Robert Fulton

All the motors so far acquired in Ireland were petrol driven, but in 1960 a diesel fuel tank was installed at Belfast and diesel vehicles ordered, all Karrier Bantams: a tractor, two covered vans and a platform lorry. At the same time petrol Karriers were also ordered, the management not being entirely convinced of the diesel's value for short-haul work. For one thing a diesel, particularly a small one, was more expensive to build because of its necessarily robust construction, and few small ones were available anyway. Moreover, its slow acceleration, coupled with its noise and smoke, made it less suitable for the stops and starts of town deliveries. Finally, its undoubted economy on long runs would not be so evident on short ones, where the petrol engine continued to show advantages of cleanliness and acceleration.

This fairly large scale motor programme was necessary because the management had by the late nineteen-fifties decided to give up horses, although as late as 1958 the few horses at Londonderry were still making a profit. By the end of that year there were only twelve horses at Belfast and eleven at Derry. The rival Cowan & Co. had given up their horses in Belfast in 1957, but Wordie's hung on at Belfast until the spring of 1960 and at Londonderry until April, 1961. It was sad for all when the horses went; many were doubtless convinced they still had a future, for other Belfast carters were keeping them—in 1962 John Harkness had forty-five.

Horses had served the Wordies well for 119 years, from 1842 when William Wordie signed his first contract with the Edinburgh & Glasgow Railway to 1961. Brutal economics were the cause of their demise: the time needed to look after them, evenings and weekends; the time they were standing, costing plenty to feed but not earning; their slow movement. Cost of feed had indeed become a burden; in 1955 the price of oats delivered from Scotland to Belfast was £33 10s (£33.50) a ton; a fair sum then, not far short of a month's wages. If a large number of horses had been kept at work then their economic standing would have looked better, with feed imported in greater bulk at cheaper rates and with stablemen, horseshoers and saddlers kept in full employ. Once their numbers were run down they showed up worse on the balance sheets, and the only solution was their complete withdrawal.

Meanwhile there were developments on the cartage contract front. In April, 1958, Mr Fyfe had reported that the Great Northern Railway Board had given notice that Wordie (Ulster)'s contract with them would expire on 30th September, 1958. This meant the end of railway work and the loss of as much as 30 per cent of the company's cartage and haulage revenue, but the board were not unduly cast down because this work was less rewarding than others, so the net profit would not suffer too seriously.

Nevertheless there was a feeling that the company could be disposed of to the Ulster Transport Authority, who were to take over the railways of the GNR Board in the province on 1st October, 1958. This hope of a sale to the UTA persisted but was never fulfilled, and in fact Wordie's continued on railway work for the UTA well beyond 1958, at Londonderry into 1963, at Belfast somewhat longer. But in 1958/59 disposal of the business was uppermost in the board's mind, partly because the future did not look promising, partly because of the difficulties of operation. By this time the chairman, Sir James Wordie, was unwell and his sons had other careers and interests. There was no possibility of building the company up into a great business like the old Wordie & Co.; the transport climate of Ulster was against that.

Rather it was a case of hanging on and making the best of the traffic that offered. In the autumn of 1959 the business was advertised for sale, but there was no serious response. In late 1961 an approach to Coast Lines of Liverpool, at that time intent on expanding their road interests, was considered, while in 1964 there were discussions with the Transport Development Group, a holding company for an ever-increasing number of road haulage operators.

In September, 1959, Sir James's second son George had been made a director and the third son Peter was to follow him on to the board in November, 1961. But Sir James died on 16th January, 1962, and his eldest son John succeeded him as chairman of the Ulster company. During the nineteen-sixties it was Wordie (Ulster) policy to battle on as best they could, with sale or amalgamation always at the back of their minds. There had been a change of management in Northern Ireland in May, 1961, when Mr Peter Dallas retired after sixty years' service, to be succeeded by Mr Joseph Duke, who worked hard to obtain new business.

Containers and roll-on, roll-off ferries were becoming recognized as the transport pattern of the future, with less reliance on old-fashioned cartage. Peter Wordie, himself in shipping, reported on a proposed service from Ardrossan to Belfast by the Atlantic Steam Navigation Company, established as vehicle ferry operators between Preston and Larne. Another interest was in Coast Lines' Link Line container service between Liverpool and Belfast. Moreover this was a time when industry was investing in Ulster; if it was to flourish a road haulage company had to break into this atmosphere of enterprise, and Mr Duke tried hard. Thus in 1965 he reported on a possible freight contract with British European Airways, while Peter Wordie had received an inquiry from Clark's Shoes, of Street in Somerset, regarding the delivery of air-freighted footwear in Northern Ireland. Unfortunately nothing came of either proposal. More promising was an approach from

Robert Fulton in the office at Divis Street, Belfast, where he was foreman.
Robert Fulton

British Rail regarding a joint Wordie-Cowan agency to handle the containers coming off the Heysham steamers; this was a chance for considerable expansion and did eventually emerge as the consortium Belfast Terminals, of which more later.

Sadly, in April, 1965, came the death of the company secretary, David Taylor. Latterly he had been acting jointly with Mr Iain Gilchrist in this capacity; Iain Gilchrist continued alone. On a happier note, Mr Duke became a director in 1965. More optimistic, too, was the future of the company. There had been some doubt about the future of the depot at Londonderry after the railway work had gone, but Mr Duke had succeeded in finding trunk loads, by that time sanctioned, between Belfast and Derry; an average of four such loads a week, with some return cargo too. Not only was Londonderry kept but there were ideas of opening outstations again, although they came to nothing.

Then came the break-up of the Ulster Transport Authority and the creation from 1st April, 1967, of two authorities, Northern Ireland Railways Co. Ltd to look after the railways only and the Northern Ireland Transport Holding Company to take care of road services; the latter was divided into Ulsterbus for the buses and Northern Ireland Carriers for the goods vehicles. The latter joined Wordie's and Cowan's at the end of 1967 to form Belfast Terminals Ltd to handle British Rail's cartage in the province.

Although it got off to a good start Belfast Terminals proved a disappointment, as did Wordie (Ulster)'s involvement with Western Ferries, a company created in 1967 to challenge Mac-Brayne's in the West Coast of Scotland trade. In 1970 the association with Cowan & Co. was carried further by a merger with the historic rival and the creation of a new company, Wordie Cowan Ltd. This amalgamation, which included a third carrier, W. M. Fleming & Co. (Carriers) Ltd, took effect on 1st April, 1970, and was followed by the sale of the share capital of Wordie (Ulster) to Wordie Cowan.

This was the end of the Wordie family's participation in road transport, although the Ulster company continued in being to 1972. However, the name Wordie linked with Cowan remained on the streets of Belfast and Londonderry until the nineteen-eighties, when the merged company merged yet again into Williames Transport and Northern Ireland Carriers.

A young Joe Galway and his lorry outside Blackstaff flax mill in Conway Street, Belfast, in 1944. He has a load of clay from Toomebridge, at the foot of Lough Neagh, to be used for boiler and pipe lagging. Mary Galway.

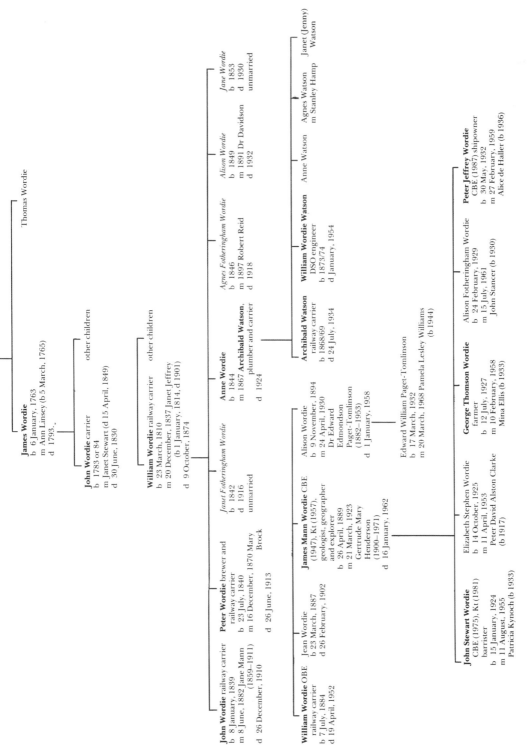

Thomas Wordie

James Wordie
b 6 January, 1763
m Ann Linsey (b 5 March, 1765)
d 1793.

John Wordie carrier
b 1783 or 84
m Janet Stewart (d 15 April, 1849)
d 30 June, 1830

other children

William Wordie railway carrier
b 23 March, 1810
m 20 December, 1837 Janet Jeffrey
(b 1 January, 1814, d 1901)
d 9 October, 1874

other children

John Wordie railway carrier
b 8 January, 1839
m 8 June, 1882 Jane Mann
(1859–1911)
d 26 December, 1910

Peter Wordie brewer and
railway carrier
b 23 July, 1840
m 16 December, 1870 Mary
Brock
d 26 June, 1913

Janet Fotheringham Wordie
b 1842
d 1916
unmarried

Anne Wordie
b 1844
m 1867 **Archibald Watson**.
plumber and carrier
d 1924

Agnes Fotheringham Wordie
b 1846
m 1897 Robert Reid
d 1918

Alison Wordie
b 1849
m 1891 Dr Davidson
d 1932

Jane Wordie
b 1853
d 1930
unmarried

William Wordie OBE
railway carrier
b 7 July, 1884
d 19 April, 1952

Jean Wordie
b 23 March, 1887
d 26 February, 1902

James Mann Wordie CBE
(1947), Kt (1957).
geologist, geographer
and explorer
b 26 April, 1889
m 21 March, 1923
Gertrude Mary
Henderson
(1900–1971)
d 16 January, 1962

Alison Wordie
b 9 November, 1894
m 24 April, 1930
Dr Edward
Edmondson
Paget-Tomlinson
(1882–1953)
d 1 January, 1958

Edward William Paget-Tomlinson
b 17 March, 1932
m 20 March, 1968 Pamela Lesley Williams
(b 1944)

Archibald Watson
railway carrier
b 1868/69
d 24 July, 1934

William Wordie Watson
DSO engineer
b 1873/74
d January, 1954

Anne Watson

Agnes Watson
m Stanley Hamp

Janet (Jenny)
Watson

John Stewart Wordie
CBE (1975), Kt (1981)
barrister
b 15 January, 1924
m 11 August, 1955
Patricia Kynoch (b 1933)

Elizabeth Stephen Wordie
b 14 October, 1925
m 11 April, 1953
Peter David Alston Clarke
(b 1917)

George Thomson Wordie
farmer
b 12 July, 1927
m 10 February, 1958
Mina Ellis (b 1933)

Alison Fotheringham Wordie
b 24 February, 1929
m 15 July, 1961
John Stancer (b 1930)

Peter Jeffrey Wordie
CBE (1987) shipowner
b 30 May, 1932
m 27 February, 1959
Alice de Haller (b 1936)

People named in text in **bold**.
People mentioned in text in *italics*.

APPENDIX TWO

Company Structure

Head Office: Glasgow

District Offices: Glasgow
Stirling
Leith
Dundee
Perth
Aberdeen
Inverness
Kirkcudbright (a later addition)
Newcastle-upon-Tyne
Belfast
Londonderry
Dublin

The local depots came under the District Offices; thus under the District Manager at Perth were:
Blairgowrie
Coupar Angus
Alyth
Aberfeldy
Pitlochry
Dunkeld
Auchterarder

Here is the structure of a district Office, Aberdeen, and a large depot with
horses and motors, Dock Street, Dundee:

The Staff of the Aberdeen District Office, Schoolhill, Aberdeen, in the nineteen-thirties recalled by
Mr Fred Gunn and Mr Fred Middleton. Others such as Inverness were similar.

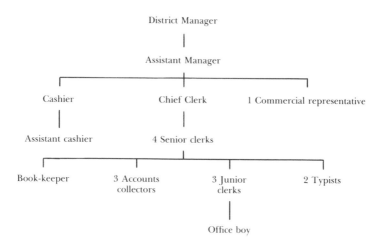

The staff of the Mid Stables, Dock Street, Dundee, in the nineteen-thirties recalled by Mr George
Philp.

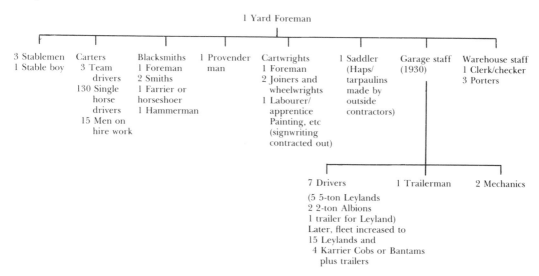

In 1946 the company structure was as follows:

Wordie & Co. Ltd, Head Office, Glasgow

District Office, Glasgow	Depot	Airdrie
District Office, Aberdeen	Depot	Stonehaven
District Office, Dundee	Depots	Arbroath
		Brechin
		Forfar
		Kirriemuir
		Montrose
District Office, Inverness	Depots	Alness
		Avoch
		Beauly
		Brora
		Burghead
		Dingwall
		Dornoch
		Elgin
		Evanton
		Fochabers
		Forres
		Fort George
		Fortrose
		Golspie
		Grantown-on-Spey
		Helmsdale
		Hopeman
		Invergordon
		Keith
		Kingussie
		Kyle of Lochalsh
		Lybster
		Nairn
		Strathpeffer
		Tain
		Thurso
		Wick
District Office, Kirkcudbright	Depots	New Galloway
		Newton Stewart
		Stranraer
District Office, Leith	Depot	Edinburgh
District Office, Perth	Depots	Aberfeldy
		Alyth
		Auchterarder
		Blairgowrie
		Coupar Angus
		Dunkeld
		Pitlochry
District Office, Stirling	Depots	Alloa
		Bannockburn
		Bonnybridge
		Denny
		Dunblane
		Falkirk
		Larbert

Wordie & Co. (Ulster) Ltd. Head Offices, Glasgow and Belfast
District Office, Belfast   Depots   Antrim
Armagh
Ballymena
Ballymoney
Coleraine
Dungannon
Enniskillen
Larne
Limavady
Londonderry
Newry
Omagh
Portrush
Strabane
Whitehead

This is much reduced from the company at its greatest extent before 1914.
By 1946 the Dublin and Newcastle businesses and the business in North-
east Scotland, Wordie's (North Eastern) Ltd, had gone, while some of the
Highland depots were given up. The map on the back endpapers shows all
the Wordie depots there ever were in Scotland.

*Sorely damaged though it
is, this old photograph
showing the celebrations
of the Coronation of
King Edward VII on
Fraserburgh Links is of
considerable interest. A
lorry parade formed part
of the celebrations.*
George A. Dey

APPENDIX THREE

Monetary Values

IN THIS age of inflation, when a pound is worth a tenth of what it was as recently as 1969, the quotation of nineteenth-century Wordie revenue and costs and nineteen-thirties wages is almost meaningless. However, these figures have been handed down by ledger and memory, so it is only right to record them. In 1939 a large loaf cost fourpence, or roughly 2p in decimal currency; 5lb of potatoes twopence-halfpenny, or 1p, milk twopence a pint; bananas seven for sixpence; the week's provisions for a family might cost ten shillings, or 50p. Bed and breakfast at a boarding house would cost four shillings and sixpence a night (22½p), or five shillings (25p) with an evening meal, and the minimum fare for a bus ride would be a penny. In the nineteenth century a pound a week was a fair average wage for a manual worker, when a loaf was a penny and beer a penny a pint. At the turn of the century coal was eighteen shillings a ton (90p), and there was the penny post.

An old postcard of Broad Street, Fraserburgh, at the time of the 1902 Coronation celebrations. Horses are much in evidence; motors have yet to appear here.
George A. Dey

Some Facts and Figures including Finance

IT IS OFTEN of interest to have a few statistical and financial details. These have been culled from the Wordie ledgers and accounts, the records in the Strathclyde Regional Archives, in the Mitchell Library in Glasgow, filed under the code TD-190-1 to 28, worked through by the team from the University of Glasgow preparing the City's Dictionary of Business Biography under the direction of Dr Sarah C. Orr. I have examined them too.

First some horse statistics. In 1861 Wordie's horses were distributed as follows:

Aberdeen	12	(the depot opened in 1854)
Alloa	26	(indicating the importance to Wordie's of the brewery and Hill Foots traffic. The Alloa depot had been opened in 1850, see chapter three
Denny	15	

At the beginning of the century the fishing industry at Fraserburgh, as elsewhere, depended to a great extent on horse transport.
George A. Dey

Dundee	8	(small beginnings there; the depot opened by 1856)
Glasgow	85	
Grahamston (Falkirk)	9	
Helensburgh	6	
Inverness	12	(not long opened)
Perth	8	(the depot opened by 1856)
Stirling	16	(three more than in 1860, see chapter three)

For evidence of the growth of the business, the surviving "horse book" provides the details of horse purchase, amplified by the records in the Mitchell Library, the latter providing the totals from 1881 to 1905. One

Below: *Dandy brush and curry comb; the latter was used to clean the hairs off the brush. At bottom is a comb used for mane and tail.*

feels 2,200 was on the low side for the total number of horses in 1905; add the Grierson stud of 92 and horses hired, and the figures could have approached the three thousand quoted in chapter four. Moreover, the two lists disagree.

Horses bought and some totals from 1858 to 1954:

	Bought (Horse Book)	Total (Records)		Bought (Horse Book)	Total (Records)
1858	44		1895	361	1498
1859	66		1896	323	1584
1860	40		1897	310	1700
1861	41		1898	369	1830
1862	85		1899	318	1937
1863	151		1900	310	1987
1864	80		1901	370	2080
1865	117		1902	307	2107
1866	40		1903	295	2160
1867	56		1904	284	2153
1868	50		1905	309	2200
1869	116	359	1906	322	
1870	130		1907	420	
1871	143		1908	145	
1872	128		1909	270	
1873	102		1910	294	
1874	104		1911	386	
1875	94		1912	305	
1876	116		1913	334	
1877	115		1914	279	
1878	81		1915	162	
1879	121		1916	299	
1880	114		1917	204	
1881	162	690	1918	314	
1882	108	701	1919	576	
1883	112	738	1920	39	
1884	111	749	1921	29	
1885	88	758	1922	131	
1886	108	745	1923	267	
1887	137	799	1924	209	
1888	156	842	1925	186	
1889	227	871	1926	246	
1890	196	969	1927	291	
1891	210	1073	1928	166	
1892	268	1184	1929	163	
1893	179	1216	1930	105	
1894	342	1269	1931	148	

E. W. P-T.

Henceforward the horses in the book are bought for the non London, Midland & Scottish Railway side of the business, what in 1938 became Wordie's (North Eastern) Ltd, and in 1937 Wordie & Co. (Ulster) Ltd and Wordie & Co. (Dublin). R. Grierson's horses would be recorded separately, as would those bought for the LMS side, but details have not come to light.

1932	15	13 for Belfast and 2 for North Eastern.
1933	46	35 for Belfast, 4 for Dublin and 7 for North Eastern.
1934	42	30 for Belfast, 6 for Dublin, 6 for North Eastern.
1935	56	42 for Belfast, 14 for North Eastern.
1936	23	20 for Belfast, 3 for North Eastern.
1937	35	24 for Wordie (Ulster), 6 for Wordie (Dublin), 5 for North Eastern.
1938	24	12 for Wordie (Ulster), 12 for Wordie (North Eastern).
1939	36	31 for Wordie (Ulster), 5 for Wordie (Dublin).
1940	32	All for Wordie (Ulster).
1941	39	24 for Wordie (Ulster), 3 for Wordie (Dublin), 12 for Wordie (North Eastern).
1942	11	All for Wordie (Ulster).
1943	23	15 for Wordie (Ulster), 8 for Wordie (North Eastern).
1944	25	19 for Wordie (Ulster), 6 for Wordie (North Eastern).
1945	34	31 for Wordie (Ulster), 3 for Wordie (North Eastern).
1946	14	All for Wordie (Ulster).
1947	12	All for Wordie (Ulster).
1948	9	All for Wordie (Ulster).
1949	6	All for Wordie (Ulster).
1950	6	All for Wordie (Ulster).
1951	No purchase	
1952	No purchase	
1953	3	All for Wordie (Ulster).
1954	3	All for Wordie (Ulster).

This list from the records shows the distribution of horses and vehicles through the business in 1903 and 1905, the vans being parcels vans:

	1903			1905		
	Horses	Lorries	Vans	Horses	Lorries	Vans
Aberdeen	339	320	6	320	323	6
Arbroath	71	54	1	91	66	—
Airdrie	12	12	—	10	10	—
Belfast	211	175	19	250	192	19
Dublin	62	60	6	170	61	3
Dundee	240	195	2	276	210	2
Edinburgh	126	112	2	129	111	2
Glasgow	507	353	38	501	396	37
Inverness	95	77	3	88	78	3
Leith	208	182	2	186	172	2
Newcastle	68	58	2	53	51	2
Perth	49	45	2	57	48	2
Paisley	—	—	—	11	4	1
Stirling	156	126	8	144	128	18
Stranraer	11	10	—	11	10	—

The Wordie fleet list in 1938, from the 12th November, 1938, number of *Modern Transport*:

The London, Midland & Scottish Railway Part of the Business

	Horses	Commercial Motors	Trailers	Private Cars	Motor Coaches
Wordie & Co. Ltd, Glasgow	824	164	61	18	
J. C. Brooke & Co. Ltd, Inverness	—	8	2		
Herbert Davidson Ltd, Edinburgh	—	16		2	
James Dickson (Transport) Ltd, Dumfries	—	11	1	1	3
Dumfries & Galloway (Transport) Ltd	—	10	1		
John Russell & Son (Carriers) Ltd, West Calder	—	17	7	3	
South Western Transports Ltd, Lockerbie	—	18	1	2	
Road Engines & Kerr (Haulage) Ltd	—	8	31	1	
James Walker (Glasgow) Ltd	—	5			
	824	257	104	27	5

Note: By 1938 only Wordie & Co. Ltd had horses; the subsidiaries were recent acquisitions, entirely motor fleets, except for Road Engines & Kerr, who had six steam traction engines in 1938 and a large fleet of low loading trailers for heavy haulage. The cars were for the use of the management but could double as service vehicles. The three or possibly five buses have so far eluded identification; the figures given are exactly as in *Modern Transport*—it is not known if one or other is a misprint or if there is a figure two missing from the list.

The Businesses Remaining under Family Control

	Horses	Commercial Motors	Trailers	Private Cars	Motor Coaches
R. Grierson & Co. Ltd, Glasgow	36	4	3	1	
Wordie & Co., Dublin	46	3	—	1	
Wordie & Co. (Ulster) Ltd	140	10	3	1	
Wordie's (North Eastern) Ltd	38	2	3		
	260	19	9	3	

Grand Totals

	Horses	Commercial Motors	Trailers	Private Cars	Motor Coaches
Railway business	824	257	104	27	? 5
Family business	260	19	9	3	—
	1084	276	113	30	? 5

Here, finally, are some balance sheets for 1869, 1872–73 and for 1924–29.

1. The earlier ones are divided into the depots or "stations". The profits do not seem to have been great in 1869, but better in 1872–73, while in the nineteen-twenties they fluctuated from a good profit in 1924 to a sizeable loss for those days in 1929.

The profit and loss figures for Ireland are separate. This was before the 1932 agreement when the London, Midland & Scottish Railway took a 51% stake in the major part of the business, as described in chapter nine.

2. Finally a breakdown of nineteen-twenties expenditure, but this time excluding the ex-Great North of Scotland stations which in 1938 came under the control of Wordie's (North Eastern) Ltd, remaining under direct family control. It seems to have always been profitable.

Grooming

1. Balance Sheets of Wordie's Main Stations

1869	Total Revenue £	Total Expenditure £	Wages £	No. of Horses
Aberdeen	5361	5678	1774	46
Arbroath	2367	2400	942	24
Dundee	4991	5170	4870	40
Edinburgh	8856	3783	1202	40
Forfar	1099	986	1058	27
Glasgow	15217	16160	1709	116
Perth	3209	2569	894	22
Stirling	1724	1055	578	14
Inverness	4082	3460	1058	30
Totals	46906	41261	14085	359

1872/3				
Aberdeen	10651	11092	3740	—
Arbroath	2961	2938	1201	—
Dundee	7981	7142	2777	—
Edinburgh	5816	5021	1885	—
Forfar	1517	1379	584	—
Glasgow	26019	24300	8188	—
Perth	3812	2889	1085	—
Stirling	2073	2241	765	—
Inverness	5602	4268	1355	—
Totals	66432	61270	21580	—

Profit and Loss Accounts, 1924–29

	1924 £	1925 £	1926 £	1927 £	1928 £	1929 £
Carting expenses	397,663	398,581	369,394	366,849	383,578	369,222
Cartage revenue	404,051	397,278	370,066	374,172	386,927	370,545
Profit from motors	3,020	3,261	2,459	2,118	3,172	3,622
Profit from storages	5,267	3,421	4,920	4,076	1,456	−15
Total Profit/ Loss for year	12,795	−384	1,902	7,729	1,762	−2,942

These figures include work for the former Great North of Scotland Railway, but not the Irish businesses or R. Grierson & Co.

Northern Ireland

	1924	1925	1926	1927	1928	1929
Profit for year	2,944	−6,474	2,986	2,319	525	87

Eire

Profit for year	−778	184	148	1,683	1,715	1,920

2. Breakdown of expenditure (excluding the work for the former Great North of Scotland Railway, the Irish businesses and R. Grierson)

	1924	1925	1926	1927	1928	1929	1930
Horse feed	59,642	59,796	53,555	45,279	52,565	54,108	44,069
Stabling	17,297	16,735	16,423	16,435	17,005	16,695	15,471
Shoeing and vet	11,698	11,781	10,991	11,052	11,186	10,771	10,228
Wages	143,665	143,207	131,167	130,884	134,111	128,499	121,729
Management	22,813	22,724	22,183	22,981	22,061	21,160	20,967
General charges	19,658	22,122	22,628	21,955	24,825	23,324	22,459
Repairs to stock	22,808	21,330	18,866	18,840	19,660	18,390	16,431

Glossary

THIS could be a vast compilation beset with pitfalls, but no attempt has been made to present a complete glossary of the transport industry; it aspires only to explain words in the text which could cause the reader to stumble. The author agrees there are many omissions, but where does one stop in a subject like this?

Benches	Platforms in a railway goods station.
Blinds	Scots word for blinkers.
Brecham	Scots word for collar, the peaked or peakit brecham being the Scottish peaked collar, also called the tappit (crested) brecham and the Glasgow pike.
Brig	Bridge on the saddle.
C & D	Collect-and-deliver traffic, see chapter seven.
Cartwright	Cart and lorry builder and repairer, in England wheelwright.
Cassies or causies	Granite setts, hard-wearing road surfacing.
Choke rail	The low rail bordering the platform of a motor lorry.
Chop house	Where the horse feed is prepared.
Cogs	Studs fitted to horseshoes for icy conditions, also called pikes.
Constantmen	Men permanently employed (Belfast); see also Spellmen.
Coup cart	Tip cart; coup is the Scots word for tip.
Darg	Daily stint of work, an old term.
Dodie	Non-peaked collar, a term used in North-east Scotland.
Dodie hames	Low hames to go with the dodie collar.
Doubles	Pair of horses, a team.
Drachts	Draught chains.
Drum horse	Horse with rheumatoid arthritis of the back legs.
Dwang	Lever for tightening securing chains, say round a load of timber; also called a sylvester.
Glasgow jock	Fibre used to make the ties or securing ropes for horse lorry haps or covers.
Glasgow pike	see Brecham.
Gyp horse	Irish gyp horse, a cross between an Irish Draught horse and a Connemara, say 15.3 to 16 hands.
Hap	Tarpaulin cover for the load on a horse or motor lorry.

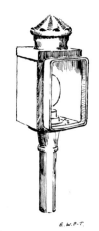

E.W.P-T.

A candle-lit cart lamp. The candle was held within a tube and seated on a spring which pushed it up as the wick and wax burnt away, so that the position of the flame remained constant in relation to the reflector.

E.W.P-T.

Hapmaker	Cover maker.
Heading board	Upright board at the front of the platform of a motor lorry.
Headstall	Bridle.
Hig	Instruction to the horse to turn left (Aberdeen).
Hip	Instruction to the horse to move forward (Aberdeen).
Irish collar	Open collar which buckles at the top, also called an Ulster collar.
Janker	see Monkey.
Kibbled	Broken corn.
Kist	Scots word for a meal bin; literally a chest.
Lead rope	Scots word for a halter.
Linen van	Van with a canvas cover or tilt.
Monkey	Four-wheeled pole vehicle with adjustable rear axle for long loads like timber, pipes or ironwork; also called a janker. This is the horse-drawn monkey; the motor equivalent bears the front of the load on a radial mounting on the lorry platform, the rear being carried by an axle secured only to the load.
Pikes	See Cogs.
Rake	Journey; so many rakes a day; an old word.
Reist	To stop a horse moving; what the secret societies were able to do.
Rigwiddy	Back chain, the Central Scottish term; but rigwoddy or rigwoodie in North-east Scotland.
S to S	Station-to-station traffic, see chapter seven.
Shoer	Horseshoer or farrier.
Sinker	Ulster term for the wooden ball at the end of the halter rope.
Smalls	Small consignments, see chapter seven.
Spellmen	Men casually employed (Belfast); see also Constant-men.
Stank	Triangular drawbar of a motor lorry's trailer.
Tappit brecham	See Brecham.
Theats	Draught chains, certainly a Glasgow term.
Tilt	Canvas cover of a van; see Linen van.
Trams	Shafts.
Troch	Water trough.
Ulster collar	see Irish collar.
Wattery chain	The chain of a curb bit, which goes under the chin; see chapter five.
Wish	An instruction to the horse to turn right (Aberdeen).

Above: *Putting collars on was a delicate business, as they had to go over the head upside down and be turned on the neck. The Ulster collar overcame this problem; it could be opened by undoing two straps at the top, these being protected by a leather flap when the collar was being worn.*

Bibliography and Sources

THE Strathclyde Regional Archives in the Mitchell Library, North Street, Glasgow, contain material relative to Wordie & Co., catalogue numbers TD-190-1–28. They include ledgers, balance sheets, correspondence received from the company, all worth studying for a picture of a cartage business at work. The following books have also been consulted in the preparation of this history and have helped to varying degrees.

Baldwin, Nick   *The Illustrated History of Albion Vehicles.* Haynes, 1988.

Baldwin, Nick   *The Illustrated History of Leyland Trucks.* Haynes, 1986.

Bonavia, Michael   *The Four Great Railways.* David and Charles, 1980.

Casserley, H. C.   *Outline of Irish Railway History.* David and Charles, 1974.

Cornwell, E. L.   *Commercial Road Vehicles.* Batsford, 1960.

Evans, George Ewart (ill. C. F. Tunnicliffe) *The Horse in the Furrow.* Faber and Faber, 1960.

Geary, Les   *Railway Road Vehicles.* Ian Henry Publications, 1987.

Holden, Bryan   *The Long Haul. The Life and Times of the Railway Horse.* J. A. Allen, 1985.

Ingram, Arthur   *Horse Drawn Vehicles since 1760.* Blandford, 1977.

Keegan, Terry   *The Heavy Horse, its Harness and Decoration.* Pelham Books, 1973.

Klapper, C. F.   *British Lorries, 1900–45.* Ian Allan, 1973.

MacTaggart, T.   *Pioneers of Heavy Haulage* (the History of Road Engines and Kerr Ltd). Alloway Publishing, 1985.

Marshall, P. and Bishop, D.   *Lorries, Trucks and Vans, 1897–1927.* Blandford, 1977.

Middlemass, Tom   *Irish Standard Gauge Railways.* David and Charles, 1981.

Millar, G. I.   *Fifty Years of Public Service* (Northern Ireland buses). Privately published, 1985.

Norris, William   *Modern Steam Road Wagons.* Longmans, 1906; reprinted David and Charles, 1971.

Patterson, E. M.   *The Great Northern Railway of Ireland.* The Oakwood Press, 1962; reprinted 1986.

Stevens-Stratten, S. W. and Aldridge, W. J.   *Railway Owned Commercial Vehicles.* Ian Allan, 1987.

Thomas, John   *A Regional History of the Railways of Great Britain, Vol. 6, Scotland, the Lowlands and the Borders.* David and Charles, 1971. Revised and enlarged by Alan J. V. Paterson, David St John Thomas, 1984.

Tuckett, Angela   *The Scottish Carter. The History of the Scottish Horse and Motormen's Association.* Allen and Unwin, 1967.

Youatt, William   *The Horse. With a Treatise on Draught.* Chapman and Hall, 1843.

Index

Illustrations in **bold type**

176

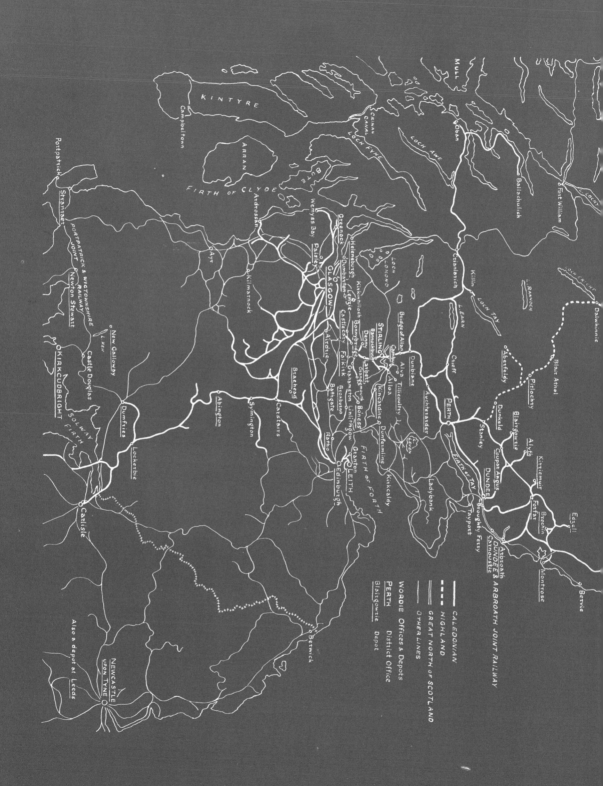

KINTYRE

Campbeltown

ARRAN

BUTE

FIRTH OF CLYDE

Portpatrick

Stranraer

PORTPATRICK & WIGTOWNSHIRE JOINT RAILWAY
Newton Stewart

L. Ken

Castle Douglas
o New Galloway

KIRKCUDBRIGHT

SOLWAY FIRTH

Dumfries

Lockerbie

Carlisle

Also a depot at Leeds

NEWCASTLE UPON TYNE

Berwick

Abington

Symington

Carstairs

Braehead

Ayr

Kilmarnock

Wemyss Bay

Ardrossan

GLASGOW

Paisley

Greenock
Helensburgh
Dumbarton
Central
Kirkintilloch
Bonnybridge
Bathgate
Bo'ness
Bathgate
Ratho
Grangemouth
Linlithgow
Granton
LEITH
EDINBURGH

FIRTH of FORTH

FALKIRK

STIRLING
Bannockbank
Denny
Larbert
Cambus
Alloa
Bridge of Allan
Tillicoultry
Kincardine
Dunfermline
Kirkcaldy
Dunblane

Ladybank

Crieff

L. LOMOND
L. EARN

Callander

LOCH LONG
LOCH FYNE
CRINAN CANAL

LOCH AWE

Oban

MULL

Ballachulish

Fort William

L. RANNOCH
LOCH TAY

Killin

Dunkeld
Auchterarder
PERTH
Stanley

FIRTH of TAY

Blairgowrie
Coupar Angus
DUNDEE
Broughty Ferry
Tayport

DUNDEE & ARBROATH JOINT RAILWAY

Arbroath
Carnoustie

Alyth
Kirriemuir
Forfar
Brechin

Montrose

Bervie

Edzell

Aberfeldy

Pitlochry

Blair Athol

Dalwhinnie

LOCH ERICHT

CALEDONIAN
HIGHLAND
GREAT NORTH OF SCOTLAND
OTHER LINES

WORDIE Offices & Depots
PERTH District Office
Blairgowrie Depot